I Have, Who Has?

LANGUAGE ARTS

5–6

W9-ARS-107

Written by
Trisha Callella

Editor: Carla Hamaguchi
Cover Illustrator: Corbin Hillam
Production: Moonhee Pak and Carrie Rickmond
Designer: Moonhee Pak
Art Director: Tom Cochrane

Table of Contents

I HAVE, WHO HAS

I HAVE, WHO HAS is a series of books that provide interactive group activities. The activities consist of game cards that students read and interactively answer. Each card game consists of 40 cards. The game starts when a student reads the first card. The student who has the card with the answer reads his or her card. The game continues in this manner until the last card is read. The last card's question "loops" back to the first card.

This book provides a fun, interactive way for students to practice various language arts skills. This resource includes over 35 card games that will improve students' listening skills and teach standards-based skills and strategies. The skills covered include:

- Synonyms
- Antonyms
- Homophones
- Compound Words
- Grammar
- Prefixes and Suffixes
- Greek and Latin Roots
- Syllabication
- Rhyming Words
- Multiple-Meaning Words
- Context Clues
- Fact or Opinion
- Vocabulary

Each game also features an active listening and enrichment activity. This component gives students practice in active listening and extends their learning to the application level.

Even better is the fact that there is hardly any prep work required to start these games in your class. Simply make copies of the game cards, cut them apart, and you are ready to go! These engaging games will keep students entertained as they are learning valuable language arts skills.

Getting Started

ORGANIZATION

There are 40 reproducible cards for each game. The cards are arranged in columns (top to bottom) in the order they will be read by the class. A reproducible active listening and enrichment page follows every set of game cards. The interactive card games for reviewing skills and strategies can be used alone or in conjunction with this reproducible page to have students practice active listening, increase active participation, provide enrichment, and extend and transfer the learning and accountability of each student.

INSTRUCTIONS FOR I HAVE, WHO HAS GAME CARDS

1) Photocopy two sets of the game cards. (Each game has four pages of 10 cards each.)

2) Cut apart one set of game cards. Mix up the cards. Pass out at least one card to each student. (There are 40 cards to accommodate large class sizes. If your class size is less than 40, then some students will have two cards. The important thing is that every student has at least one card.)

3) Keep one copy of the game cards as your reference to the correct order. The cards are printed in order in columns from top to bottom and left to right.

4) Have the student with the first game card begin the game by saying *I have the first card. Who has . . . ?* As each student reads a card, monitor your copy to make sure students are reading the cards in the correct order. If students correctly matched each card, then the last card read will "loop" back to the first card.

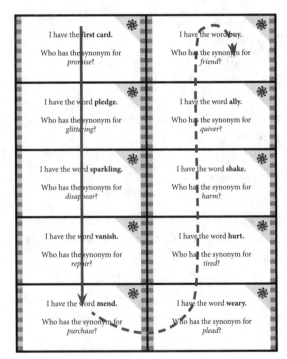

INSTRUCTIONS FOR ACTIVE LISTENING & ENRICHMENT PAGE

1) This page is optional and is not necessary to play the game.

2) Copy one page for each student or pair of students.

3) Make sure each student has a light-colored crayon or highlighter (not a marker or pencil) to color over the correct boxes as they are read.

4) As each matching card is read, provide time for students to highlight or lightly color in the correct box. If the game is slow for a particular class, two children can help each other with one reproducible page.

5) After the last card is read ("Who has the first card?"), ask students to uncover the hidden text (e.g., riddle, proverb) by reading the text in all the boxes they did not highlight or color. Have them read from top to bottom and from left to right on the grid. Then, have them answer the extension questions at the bottom of the page.

6) Use the answer key on pages 201–204 to check students' answers.

WHAT TO WATCH FOR

1) Students who have difficulty locating the correct boxes on the active listening and enrichment page after the first game (establish familiarity with the format) may have visual discrimination difficulties.

2) Students who have difficulty reading their card at the correct time may have difficulties with attention, hearing, active listening, or the concepts being reinforced.

VARIATIONS

Timed Version

1) Follow the instructions to prepare the game cards so that each student has at least one. Play without the reproducible page. Tell students that they will play the game twice. Challenge them to beat their time in the second round.

2) Have students play the same game again the next day. Can they beat their time again? Remember to mix up the cards and redistribute them before each game.

3) The more students play, the better they will understand the concepts covered in each game. They will also develop stronger phrasing and fluency in reading.

Small Groups

1) Photocopy one set of game cards (four pages, 40 cards total) for each small group. Play without the reproducible page.

2) Cut apart the cards, mix them up, and give a set to each group.

3) Have each group play. You can time the groups to encourage them to pay close attention, read quickly, and stay on task. Which group is the fastest?

4) By playing in smaller groups, each student has more cards. This raises the individual accountability, activity, time on task, and reinforcement opportunities per student.

Synonyms 1

I have the **first card.**

Who has the synonym for *abandon*?

I have the word **educate.**

Who has the synonym for *bother*?

I have the word **leave.**

Who has the synonym for *hungry*?

I have the word **disturb.**

Who has the synonym for *timid*?

I have the word **famished.**

Who has the synonym for *pretty*?

I have the word **shy.**

Who has the synonym for *understand*?

I have the word **attractive.**

Who has the synonym for *hide*?

I have the word **comprehend.**

Who has the synonym for *snooze*?

I have the word **conceal.**

Who has the synonym for *teach*?

I have the word **rest.**

Who has the synonym for *locate*?

Synonyms 1

I have the word **find.**

Who has the synonym for *dressed*?

I have the word **infamous.**

Who has the synonym for *deadly*?

I have the word **clothed.**

Who has the synonym for *silly*?

I have the word **fatal.**

Who has the synonym for *demonstrate*?

I have the word **foolish.**

Who has the synonym for *opinion*?

I have the word **show.**

Who has the synonym for *truthful*?

I have the word **viewpoint.**

Who has the synonym for *happy*?

I have the word **honest.**

Who has the synonym for *copy*?

I have the word **joyful.**

Who has the synonym for *notorious*?

I have the word **imitate.**

Who has the synonym for *ordinary*?

I Have, Who Has?: Language Arts • 5–6 © 2006 Creative Teaching Press

Synonyms 1

I have the word **plain.**

Who has the synonym for *emergency?*

I have the word **describe.**

Who has the synonym for *task?*

I have the word **crisis.**

Who has the synonym for *gigantic?*

I have the word **job.**

Who has the synonym for *abrupt?*

I have the word **huge.**

Who has the synonym for *mistake?*

I have the word **sudden.**

Who has the synonym for *attempt?*

I have the word **error.**

Who has the synonym for *section?*

I have the word **try.**

Who has the synonym for *delicious?*

I have the word **piece.**

Who has the synonym for *explain?*

I have the word **tasty.**

Who has the synonym for *late?*

I Have, Who Has?: Language Arts • 5–6 © 2006 Creative Teaching Press

Synonyms 1

I have the word **tardy.**

Who has the synonym for *help*?

I have the word **make.**

Who has the synonym for *hurry*?

I have the word **aid.**

Who has the synonym for *slow*?

I have the word **rush.**

Who has the synonym for *fortunate*?

I have the word **sluggish.**

Who has the synonym for *frequently*?

I have the word **lucky.**

Who has the synonym for *noisy*?

I have the word **often.**

Who has the synonym for *modern*?

I have the word **loud.**

Who has the synonym for *thing*?

I have the word **current.**

Who has the synonym for *create*?

I have the word **item.**

Who has the first card?

Synonyms 1

As your classmates identify each synonym, lightly color in the matching box. Listen closely so you don't miss any answers. Read the words in the remaining boxes from top to bottom and left to right to uncover the hidden proverb.

TRY	A	FOOLISH	TASTY	OFTEN
DISTURB	CRISIS	LOUD	IMITATE	SHY
MAKE	LEAVE	PENNY	PLAIN	SAVED
IS	SLUGGISH	SHOW	ATTRACTIVE	VIEWPOINT
JOYFUL	HUGE	A PENNY	TARDY	ITEM
INFAMOUS	DESCRIBE	FAMISHED	LUCKY	JOB
RUSH	EARNED	CLOTHED	ERROR	COMPREHEND
CONCEAL	FATAL	CURRENT	AID	SUDDEN
FIND	REST	PIECE	EDUCATE	HONEST

Write the proverb you uncovered.

_____

Write two synonyms for the third word of the proverb.

_____   _____

Write two synonyms for the last word of the proverb.

_____   _____

I Have, Who Has?: Language Arts • 5–6 © 2006 Creative Teaching Press

Synonyms 2

I have the **first card.**

Who has the synonym for
promise?

I have the word **buy.**

Who has the synonym for
friend?

I have the word **pledge.**

Who has the synonym for
glittering?

I have the word **ally.**

Who has the synonym for
quiver?

I have the word **sparkling.**

Who has the synonym for
disappear?

I have the word **shake.**

Who has the synonym for
harm?

I have the word **vanish.**

Who has the synonym for
repair?

I have the word **hurt.**

Who has the synonym for
tired?

I have the word **mend.**

Who has the synonym for
purchase?

I have the word **weary.**

Who has the synonym for
plead?

Synonyms 2

I have the word **beg.**

Who has the synonym for *attempt*?

I have the word **scared.**

Who has the synonym for *caution*?

I have the word **try.**

Who has the synonym for *enormous*?

I have the word **warn.**

Who has the synonym for *odor*?

I have the word **immense.**

Who has the synonym for *answer*?

I have the word **smell.**

Who has the synonym for *apparel*?

I have the word **respond.**

Who has the synonym for *nearby*?

I have the word **clothing.**

Who has the synonym for *remember*?

I have the word **close.**

Who has the synonym for *afraid*?

I have the word **recall.**

Who has the synonym for *peculiar*?

I Have, Who Has?: Language Arts • 5–6 © 2006 Creative Teaching Press

Synonyms 2

I have the word **strange.**

Who has the synonym for
terrible?

I have the word **easy.**

Who has the synonym for
fearless?

I have the word **awful.**

Who has the synonym for
govern?

I have the word **brave.**

Who has the synonym for
desire?

I have the word **rule.**

Who has the synonym for
dense?

I have the word **want.**

Who has the synonym for
start?

I have the word **thick.**

Who has the synonym for
intelligent?

I have the word **begin.**

Who has the synonym for
blend?

I have the word **smart.**

Who has the synonym for
simple?

I have the word **mix.**

Who has the synonym for
complete?

Synonyms 2

I have the word **finish.**

Who has the synonym for
sadness?

I have the word **grief.**

Who has the synonym for
depart?

I have the word **leave.**

Who has the synonym for
laughable?

I have the word **hilarious.**

Who has the synonym for
demolish?

I have the word **destroy.**

Who has the synonym for
moist?

I have the word **damp.**

Who has the synonym for
identical?

I have the word **matching.**

Who has the synonym for
select?

I have the word **choose.**

Who has the synonym for
assist?

I have the word **help.**

Who has the synonym for
leap?

I have the word **jump.**

Who has the first card?

I Have, Who Has?: Language Arts • 5–6 © 2006 Creative Teaching Press

Synonyms 2

As your classmates identify each synonym, lightly color in the matching box. Listen closely so you don't miss any answers. Read the words in the remaining boxes from top to bottom and left to right to uncover the hidden proverb.

AWFUL	EASY	SMELL	HELP	TRY
PLEDGE	RECALL	GRIEF	SHAKE	BRAVE
MIX	SPARKLING	CHOOSE	FINISH	LEAVE
WARN	DESTROY	CLOTHING	IMMENSE	MATCHING
AN APPLE	STRANGE	BEG	THICK	MEND
RULE	A DAY	BUY	SCARED	BEGIN
WEARY	VANISH	DAMP	RESPOND	HILARIOUS
KEEPS	SMART	WANT	JUMP	CLOSE
THE	HURT	DOCTOR	ALLY	AWAY

Write the proverb you uncovered.

_____

Write two synonyms for the fifth word of the proverb.

_____   _____

Write two synonyms for your favorite word from the list above. Favorite word: _____

_____   _____

Synonyms 3

I have the **first card.**

Who has the synonym for *delicate?*

I have the word **achieve.**

Who has the synonym for *curve?*

I have the word **fragile.**

Who has the synonym for *banquet?*

I have the word **bend.**

Who has the synonym for *gather?*

I have the word **feast.**

Who has the synonym for *occasion?*

I have the word **collect.**

Who has the synonym for *artificial?*

I have the word **event.**

Who has the synonym for *boast?*

I have the word **fake.**

Who has the synonym for *purchase?*

I have the word **brag.**

Who has the synonym for *accomplish?*

I have the word **buy.**

Who has the synonym for *couple?*

I Have, Who Has: Language Arts • 5–6 © 2006 Creative Teaching Press

Synonyms 3

I have the word **pair.**

Who has the synonym for *diminish*?

I have the word **copy.**

Who has the synonym for *injure*?

I have the word **decrease.**

Who has the synonym for *fret*?

I have the word **harm.**

Who has the synonym for *affluent*?

I have the word **worry.**

Who has the synonym for *debate*?

I have the word **wealthy.**

Who has the synonym for *courteous*?

I have the word **argue.**

Who has the synonym for *pardon*?

I have the word **polite.**

Who has the synonym for *authentic*?

I have the word **excuse.**

Who has the synonym for *replicate*?

I have the word **genuine.**

Who has the synonym for *decide*?

I Have, Who Has?: Language Arts • 5–6 © 2006 Creative Teaching Press

Synonyms 3

I have the word **choose**.

Who has the synonym for *acquire*?

I have the word **brave**.

Who has the synonym for *bashful*?

I have the word **obtain**.

Who has the synonym for *communicate*?

I have the word **timid**.

Who has the synonym for *melancholy*?

I have the word **discuss**.

Who has the synonym for *portion*?

I have the word **depression**.

Who has the synonym for *silent*?

I have the word **part**.

Who has the synonym for *defect*?

I have the word **noiseless**.

Who has the synonym for *postpone*?

I have the word **flaw**.

Who has the synonym for *courageous*?

I have the word **delay**.

Who has the synonym for *seashore*?

I Have, Who Has?: Language Arts • 5–6 © 2006 Creative Teaching Press

Synonyms 3

I have the word **beach.**

Who has the synonym for
command?

I have the word **leave.**

Who has the synonym for
tainted?

I have the word **order.**

Who has the synonym for
scream?

I have the word **contaminated.**

Who has the synonym for
deceive?

I have the word **shriek.**

Who has the synonym for
assistant?

I have the word **trick.**

Who has the synonym for
construct?

I have the word **aide.**

Who has the synonym for
journey?

I have the word **build.**

Who has the synonym for
contemplate?

I have the word **trip.**

Who has the synonym for
abandon?

I have the word **think.**

Who has the first card?

Synonyms 3

As your classmates identify each synonym, lightly color in the matching box. Listen closely so you don't miss any answers. Read the words in the remaining boxes from top to bottom and left to right to uncover the hidden proverb.

FRAGILE	COPY	PART	OBTAIN	EVENT
FLAW	CHOOSE	BEND	DEPRESSION	BRAVE
PAIR	NOISELESS	BUY	DISCUSS	TIME
LEAVE	HEALS	CONTAMINATED	WORRY	FEAST
ALL	ACHIEVE	HARM	TIMID	BUILD
BRAG	DELAY	AIDE	WOUNDS	POLITE
WEALTHY	EXCUSE	TRICK	FAKE	TRIP
THINK	BEACH	COLLECT	GENUINE	ORDER
DECREASE	SHRIEK	ARGUE	*	*

Write the proverb you uncovered.

_____

Write two synonyms for the second word of the proverb.

_____   _____

Write two synonyms for the last word of the proverb.

_____   _____

I Have, Who Has?: Language Arts • 5–6 © 2006 Creative Teaching Press

Synonyms 4

I have the **first card.**

Who has the synonym for
inexpensive?

I have the word **destroy.**

Who has the synonym for
comical?

I have the word **cheap.**

Who has the synonym for
marvelous?

I have the word **funny.**

Who has the synonym for
hazardous?

I have the word **wonderful.**

Who has the synonym for
option?

I have the word **dangerous.**

Who has the synonym for
repair?

I have the word **choice.**

Who has the synonym for
dilemma?

I have the word **fix.**

Who has the synonym for
powerful?

I have the word **problem.**

Who has the synonym for
annihilate?

I have the word **strong.**

Who has the synonym for
ailment?

I Have, Who Has?: Language Arts • 5–6 © 2006 Creative Teaching Press

Synonyms 4

I have the word **sickness.**

Who has the synonym for *observable*?

I have the word **feelings.**

Who has the synonym for *anxious*?

I have the word **visible.**

Who has the synonym for *enormous*?

I have the word **nervous.**

Who has the synonym for *depart*?

I have the word **gigantic.**

Who has the synonym for *decision*?

I have the word **leave.**

Who has the synonym for *liberty*?

I have the word **verdict.**

Who has the synonym for *uncooked*?

I have the word **freedom.**

Who has the synonym for *necessary*?

I have the word **raw.**

Who has the synonym for *emotions*?

I have the word **essential.**

Who has the synonym for *unusual*?

I Have, Who Has?: Language Arts • 5–6 © 2006 Creative Teaching Press

I have the word **odd**.

Who has the synonym for *ordinary*?

I have the word **exotic**.

Who has the synonym for *declare*?

I have the word **plain**.

Who has the synonym for *justice*?

I have the word **claim**.

Who has the synonym for *persevere*?

I have the word **fairness**.

Who has the synonym for *untrue*?

I have the word **persist**.

Who has the synonym for *conclusion*?

I have the word **false**.

Who has the synonym for *hypothesize*?

I have the word **end**.

Who has the synonym for *companion*?

I have the word **predict**.

Who has the synonym for *foreign*?

I have the word **friend**.

Who has the synonym for *employ*?

Synonyms 4

I have the word **hire.**

Who has the synonym for *discover*?

I have the word **fragile.**

Who has the synonym for *productive*?

I have the word **find.**

Who has the synonym for *expedition*?

I have the word **constructive.**

Who has the synonym for *elderly*?

I have the word **trek.**

Who has the synonym for *thankfulness*?

I have the word **aged.**

Who has the synonym for *savor*?

I have the word **gratitude.**

Who has the synonym for *browse*?

I have the word **enjoy.**

Who has the synonym for *dreary*?

I have the word **scan.**

Who has the synonym for *delicate*?

I have the word **gloomy.**

Who has the first card?

I Have, Who Has?: Language Arts • 5–6 © 2006 Creative Teaching Press

Synonyms 4

As your classmates identify each synonym, lightly color in the matching box. Listen closely so you don't miss any answers. Read the words in the remaining boxes from top to bottom and left to right to uncover the hidden proverb.

GRATITUDE	DESTROY	VERDICT	ODD	FRIEND
RAW	EXOTIC	END	TREK	CHOICE
BEAUTY	FEELINGS	GLOOMY	ESSENTIAL	ENJOY
FUNNY	IS	PROBLEM	CLAIM	GIGANTIC
ONLY	STRONG	SKIN	FIX	PREDICT
SCAN	DEEP	PLAIN	VISIBLE	FIND
SICKNESS	FRAGILE	NERVOUS	AGED	PERSIST
LEAVE	CHEAP	HIRE	FREEDOM	WONDERFUL
CONSTRUCTIVE	FALSE	FAIRNESS	DANGEROUS	*

Write the proverb you uncovered.

_____

Write two synonyms for the first word of the proverb.

_____   _____

Write two synonyms for the last word of the proverb.

_____   _____

I Have, Who Has? Language Arts • 5–6 © 2006 Creative Teaching Press

Antonyms 1

I have the **first card.**

Who has the antonym for *generous*?

I have the word **send.**

Who has the antonym for *strong*?

I have the word **greedy.**

Who has the antonym for *clockwise*?

I have the word **weak.**

Who has the antonym for *correct*?

I have the word **counterclockwise.**

Who has the antonym for *unimportant*?

I have the word **wrong.**

Who has the antonym for *ignore*?

I have the word **urgent.**

Who has the antonym for *prompt*?

I have the word **notice.**

Who has the antonym for *relaxed*?

I have the word **late.**

Who has the antonym for *receive*?

I have the word **nervous.**

Who has the antonym for *probable*?

I Have, Who Has?: Language Arts • 5–6 © 2006 Creative Teaching Press

Antonyms 1

I have the word **unlikely.**

Who has the antonym for *bloom*?

I have the word **fall.**

Who has the antonym for *closed*?

I have the word **wilt.**

Who has the antonym for *win*?

I have the word **open.**

Who has the antonym for *float*?

I have the word **lose.**

Who has the antonym for *unwrap*?

I have the word **sink.**

Who has the antonym for *impatient*?

I have the word **wrap.**

Who has the antonym for *female*?

I have the word **patient.**

Who has the antonym for *pay*?

I have the word **male.**

Who has the antonym for *rise*?

I have the word **owe.**

Who has the antonym for *trustworthy*?

Antonyms 1

I have the word **dishonest.**

Who has the antonym for *backward*?

I have the word **play.**

Who has the antonym for *repair*?

I have the word **forward.**

Who has the antonym for *purchase*?

I have the word **damage.**

Who has the antonym for *beginning*?

I have the word **sell.**

Who has the antonym for *natural*?

I have the word **ending.**

Who has the antonym for *locate*?

I have the word **synthetic.**

Who has the antonym for *republican*?

I have the word **misplace.**

Who has the antonym for *unpleasant*?

I have the word **democrat.**

Who has the antonym for *work*?

I have the word **pleasant.**

Who has the antonym for *different*?

I Have, Who Has?: Language Arts • 5–6 © 2006 Creative Teaching Press

Antonyms 1

I have the word **similar.**

Who has the antonym for *arid*?

I have the word **export.**

Who has the antonym for *renewed*?

I have the word **humid.**

Who has the antonym for *excited*?

I have the word **expired.**

Who has the antonym for *crowded*?

I have the word **bored.**

Who has the antonym for *fragile*?

I have the word **desolate.**

Who has the antonym for *treasured*?

I have the word **sturdy.**

Who has the antonym for *evening*?

I have the word **despised.**

Who has the antonym for *harmful*?

I have the word **morning.**

Who has the antonym for *import*?

I have the word **safe.**

Who has the first card?

Antonyms 1

As your classmates identify each antonym, lightly color in the matching box. Listen closely so you don't miss any answers. Read the words in the remaining boxes from top to bottom and left to right to uncover the hidden proverb.

OPEN	WRONG	FORWARD	SINK	COUNTER-CLOCKWISE
WILT	MORNING	PLAY	NOTICE	STURDY
WEAK	DISHONEST	SIMILAR	BORED	LOSE
SAFE	MISPLACE	GREEDY	DON'T	DAMAGE
PLEASANT	PUT ALL	WRAP	YOUR	PATIENT
EGGS	FALL	IN ONE	ENDING	URGENT
SEND	BASKET	DEMOCRAT	MALE	SELL
DESPISED	SYNTHETIC	EXPORT	NERVOUS	OWE
UNLIKELY	DESOLATE	LATE	EXPIRED	HUMID

Write the proverb you uncovered.

_____

Write two antonyms for the second word of the proverb.

_____   _____

Write two antonyms for the sixth word of the proverb.

_____   _____

I Have, Who Has?: Language Arts • 5–6 © 2006 Creative Teaching Press

Antonyms 2

I have the **first card.**

Who has the antonym for *closed*?

I have the word **depart.**

Who has the antonym for *irate?*

I have the word **open.**

Who has the antonym for *descend*?

I have the word **calm.**

Who has the antonym for *organized*?

I have the word **climb.**

Who has the antonym for *private*?

I have the word **messy.**

Who has the antonym for *income*?

I have the word **public.**

Who has the antonym for *unfair*?

I have the word **expense.**

Who has the antonym for *protest*?

I have the word **fair.**

Who has the antonym for *arrive*?

I have the word **support.**

Who has the antonym for *separate*?

I Have, Who Has? Language Arts • 5–6 © 2006 Creative Teaching Press

Antonyms 2

I have the word **combine.**

Who has the antonym for *heavy*?

I have the word **humble.**

Who has the antonym for *enormous*?

I have the word **light.**

Who has the antonym for *friend*?

I have the word **tiny.**

Who has the antonym for *prohibit*?

I have the word **foe.**

Who has the antonym for *last*?

I have the word **allow.**

Who has the antonym for *irresponsible*?

I have the word **first.**

Who has the antonym for *superior*?

I have the word **responsible.**

Who has the antonym for *punishment*?

I have the word **inferior.**

Who has the antonym for *boastful*?

I have the word **reward.**

Who has the antonym for *future*?

I Have, Who Has?: Language Arts • 5–6 © 2006 Creative Teaching Press

Antonyms 2

I have the word **past.**

Who has the antonym for *disagree?*

I have the word **divide.**

Who has the antonym for *happiness?*

I have the word **agree.**

Who has the antonym for *rested?*

I have the word **misery.**

Who has the antonym for *polite?*

I have the word **tired.**

Who has the antonym for *enter?*

I have the word **rude.**

Who has the antonym for *search?*

I have the word **exit.**

Who has the antonym for *endanger?*

I have the word **find.**

Who has the antonym for *synonym?*

I have the word **protect.**

Who has the antonym for *multiply?*

I have the word **antonym.**

Who has the antonym for *ungrateful?*

Antonyms 2

I have the word **thankful.**

Who has the antonym for *push*?

I have the word **pull.**

Who has the antonym for *subtract*?

I have the word **add.**

Who has the antonym for *giggle*?

I have the word **cry.**

Who has the antonym for *hairy*?

I have the word **bald.**

Who has the antonym for *throw*?

I have the word **catch.**

Who has the antonym for *unprepared*?

I have the word **ready.**

Who has the antonym for *confuse*?

I have the word **clarify.**

Who has the antonym for *unpack*?

I have the word **pack.**

Who has the antonym for *invertebrate*?

I have the word **vertebrate.**

Who has the first card?

I Have, Who Has?: Language Arts • 5–6 © 2006 Creative Teaching Press

Antonyms 2

As your classmates identify each antonym, lightly color in the matching box. Listen closely so you don't miss any answers. Read the words in the remaining boxes from top to bottom and left to right to uncover the hidden proverb.

OPEN	FIRST	EXPENSE	INFERIOR	CALM
TIRED	FIND	A FOOL	CATCH	REWARD
CLARIFY	FOE	AGREE	LIGHT	RESPONSIBLE
CLIMB	AND HIS	RUDE	PROTECT	DEPART
PULL	PAST	ALLOW	ADD	MONEY
ARE	READY	EXIT	SOON	ANTONYM
PUBLIC	SUPPORT	PARTED	COMBINE	FAIR
TINY	DIVIDE	MESSY	CRY	VERTEBRATE
THANKFUL	PACK	BALD	HUMBLE	MISERY

Write the proverb you uncovered.

_____

Write two antonyms for the second word of the proverb.

_____   _____

Write two antonyms for the last word of the proverb.

_____   _____

Antonyms 3

I have the **first card.**

Who has the antonym for *borrow*?

I have the word **fall.**

Who has the antonym for *dirty*?

I have the word **lend.**

Who has the antonym for *silence*?

I have the word **clean.**

Who has the antonym for *healthy*?

I have the word **noise.**

Who has the antonym for *impolite*?

I have the word **ill.**

Who has the antonym for *reject*?

I have the word **courteous.**

Who has the antonym for *compliment*?

I have the word **accept.**

Who has the antonym for *innocent*?

I have the word **insult.**

Who has the antonym for *rise*?

I have the word **guilty.**

Who has the antonym for *give*?

I Have, Who Has?: Language Arts • 5–6 © 2006 Creative Teaching Press

Antonyms 3

I have the word **take.**

Who has the antonym for *exciting*?

I have the word **fact.**

Who has the antonym for *liquid*?

I have the word **boring.**

Who has the antonym for *failure*?

I have the word **solid.**

Who has the antonym for *chilled*?

I have the word **success.**

Who has the antonym for *disconnect*?

I have the word **warmed.**

Who has the antonym for *difficult*?

I have the word **connect.**

Who has the antonym for *even*?

I have the word **simple.**

Who has the antonym for *loose*?

I have the word **odd.**

Who has the antonym for *fiction*?

I have the word **tight.**

Who has the antonym for *temporary*?

Antonyms 3

I have the word **permanent.**

Who has the antonym for *tame*?

I have the word **grow.**

Who has the antonym for *false*?

I have the word **wild.**

Who has the antonym for *prompt*?

I have the word **true.**

Who has the antonym for *ask*?

I have the word **tardy.**

Who has the antonym for *east*?

I have the word **answer.**

Who has the antonym for *start*?

I have the word **west.**

Who has the antonym for *summer*?

I have the word **finish.**

Who has the antonym for *work*?

I have the word **winter.**

Who has the antonym for *shrink*?

I have the word **rest.**

Who has the antonym for *inexpensive*?

I Have, Who Has?: Language Arts • 5–6 © 2006 Creative Teaching Press

Antonyms 3

I have the word **costly.**

Who has the antonym for *familiar*?

I have the word **trap.**

Who has the antonym for *youthful*?

I have the word **strange.**

Who has the antonym for *empty*?

I have the word **elderly.**

Who has the antonym for *wealthy*?

I have the word **full.**

Who has the antonym for *asleep*?

I have the word **poor.**

Who has the antonym for *build*?

I have the word **awake.**

Who has the antonym for *positive*?

I have the word **destroy.**

Who has the antonym for *narrow*?

I have the word **negative.**

Who has the antonym for *release*?

I have the word **wide.**

Who has the first card?

Antonyms 3

As your classmates identify each antonym, lightly color in the matching box. Listen closely so you don't miss any answers. Read the words in the remaining boxes from top to bottom and left to right to uncover the hidden proverb.

TARDY	LEND	WEST	GUILTY	PERMANENT
WARMED	DESTROY	SOLID	MONEY	FINISH
IS	ACCEPT	AWAKE	CLEAN	THE
STRANGE	COSTLY	ROOT	ELDERLY	TAKE
FALL	WIDE	SUCCESS	WILD	POOR
ANSWER	ILL	WINTER	OF ALL	NOISE
FULL	BORING	EVIL	TRAP	GROW
SIMPLE	NEGATIVE	CONNECT	ODD	REST
TIGHT	INSULT	TRUE	COURTEOUS	FACT

Write the proverb you uncovered.

_____

Write two antonyms for the fourth word of the proverb.

_____   _____

Write two antonyms for the last word of the proverb.

_____   _____

I Have, Who Has?: Language Arts • 5–6 © 2006 Creative Teaching Press

Antonyms 4

I have the **first card.**

Who has the antonym for *ashamed*?

I have the word **doubt.**

Who has the antonym for *smooth*?

I have the word **proud.**

Who has the antonym for *abundant*?

I have the word **rough.**

Who has the antonym for *include*?

I have the word **scarce.**

Who has the antonym for *frown*?

I have the word **omit.**

Who has the antonym for *fresh*?

I have the word **smile.**

Who has the antonym for *cautious*?

I have the word **stale.**

Who has the antonym for *victory*?

I have the word **reckless.**

Who has the antonym for *believe*?

I have the word **defeat.**

Who has the antonym for *left*?

I Have, Who Has? Language Arts • 5–6 © 2006 Creative Teaching Press

Antonyms 4

I have the word **right**.

Who has the antonym for *ancient*?

I have the word **after**.

Who has the antonym for *soft*?

I have the word **modern**.

Who has the antonym for *forbid*?

I have the word **hard**.

Who has the antonym for *cruel*?

I have the word **permit**.

Who has the antonym for *found*?

I have the word **kind**.

Who has the antonym for *quiet*?

I have the word **lost**.

Who has the antonym for *remember*?

I have the word **noisy**.

Who has the antonym for *dark*?

I have the word **forget**.

Who has the antonym for *before*?

I have the word **light**.

Who has the antonym for *mournful*?

I Have, Who Has?: Language Arts • 5–6 © 2006 Creative Teaching Press

Antonyms 4

I have the word **cheerful.**

Who has the antonym for *rush*?

I have the word **pessimistic.**

Who has the antonym for *thick*?

I have the word **delay.**

Who has the antonym for *shallow*?

I have the word **thin.**

Who has the antonym for *whole*?

I have the word **deep.**

Who has the antonym for *absent*?

I have the word **part.**

Who has the antonym for *straight*?

I have the word **present.**

Who has the antonym for *wise*?

I have the word **crooked.**

Who has the antonym for *wet*?

I have the word **foolish.**

Who has the antonym for *optimistic*?

I have the word **dry.**

Who has the antonym for *delicious*?

Antonyms 4

I have the word **flavorless.**

Who has the antonym for *thaw*?

I have the word **save.**

Who has the antonym for *separate*?

I have the word **freeze.**

Who has the antonym for *rare*?

I have the word **join.**

Who has the antonym for *rainy*?

I have the word **common.**

Who has the antonym for *never*?

I have the word **sunny.**

Who has the antonym for *uncertain*?

I have the word **always.**

Who has the antonym for *fancy*?

I have the word **definite.**

Who has the antonym for *blurry*?

I have the word **plain.**

Who has the antonym for *spend*?

I have the word **clear.**

Who has the first card?

I Have, Who Has?: Language Arts • 5–6 © 2006 Creative Teaching Press

Antonyms 4

As your classmates identify each antonym, lightly color in the matching box. Listen closely so you don't miss any answers. Read the words in the remaining boxes from top to bottom and left to right to uncover the hidden proverb.

HONESTY	DRY	PRESENT	DEFEAT	IS
STALE	FORGET	CHEERFUL	THE	LOST
BEST	PROUD	CROOKED	PLAIN	DEFINITE
FLAVORLESS	HARD	PESSIMISTIC	SCARCE	MODERN
NOISY	CLEAR	LIGHT	POLICY	PERMIT
PART	SMILE	ALWAYS	ROUGH	DEEP
RIGHT	AFTER	SAVE	DELAY	JOIN
COMMON	RECKLESS	FOOLISH	FREEZE	OMIT
SUNNY	KIND	DOUBT	THIN	*

Write the proverb you uncovered.

_____

_____

Write two antonyms for the first word of the proverb.

_____   _____

Write two antonyms for the fourth word of the proverb.

_____   _____

Contractions 1

I have the **first card.**

Who has the contraction for *it is*?

I have the contraction **he'd.**

Who has the contraction for *does not*?

I have the contraction **it's.**

Who has the contraction for *who is*?

I have the contraction **doesn't.**

Who has the contraction for *could have*?

I have the contraction **who's.**

Who has the contraction for *are not*?

I have the contraction **could've.**

Who has the contraction for *you have*?

I have the contraction **aren't.**

Who has the contraction for *that is*?

I have the contraction **you've.**

Who has the contraction for *can not*?

I have the contraction **that's.**

Who has the contraction for *he would*?

I have the contraction **can't.**

Who has the contraction for *would not*?

I Have, Who Has?: Language Arts • 5–6 © 2006 Creative Teaching Press

Contractions 1

I have the contraction
wouldn't.

Who has the contraction for
they will?

I have the contraction
she's.

Who has the contraction for
would have?

I have the contraction
they'll.

Who has the contraction for
did not?

I have the contraction
would've.

Who has the contraction for
we will?

I have the contraction
didn't.

Who has the contraction for
I am?

I have the contraction
we'll.

Who has the contraction for
they had?

I have the contraction
I'm.

Who has the contraction for
was not?

I have the contraction
they'd.

Who has the contraction for
will not?

I have the contraction
wasn't.

Who has the contraction for
she is?

I have the contraction
won't.

Who has the contraction for
they have?

Contractions 1

I have the contraction **they've.**

Who has the contraction for *I will?*

I have the contraction **I'll.**

Who has the contraction for *we have?*

I have the contraction **we've.**

Who has the contraction for *I have?*

I have the contraction **I've.**

Who has the contraction for *he is?*

I have the contraction **he's.**

Who has the contraction for *could not?*

I have the contraction **couldn't.**

Who has the contraction for *what is?*

I have the contraction **what's.**

Who has the contraction for *you had?*

I have the contraction **you'd.**

Who has the contraction for *I had?*

I have the contraction **I'd.**

Who has the contraction for *should not?*

I have the contraction **shouldn't.**

Who has the contraction for *you are?*

I Have, Who Has?: Language Arts • 5–6 © 2006 Creative Teaching Press

Contractions 1

I have the contraction
you're.

Who has the contraction for
we are?

I have the contraction
how's.

Who has the contraction for
should have?

I have the contraction
we're.

Who has the contraction for
had not?

I have the contraction
should've.

Who has the contraction for
they are?

I have the contraction
hadn't.

Who has the contraction for
do not?

I have the contraction
they're.

Who has the contraction for
what will?

I have the contraction
don't.

Who has the contraction for
you will?

I have the contraction
what'll.

Who has the contraction for
who will?

I have the contraction
you'll.

Who has the contraction for
how is?

I have the contraction
who'll.

Who has the first card?

Contractions 1

As your classmates identify each contraction, lightly color in the matching box. Listen closely so you don't miss any answers. Read the words in the remaining boxes from top to bottom and left to right to uncover the hidden proverb.

WE'VE	WHO'LL	SHOULDN'T	THEY'VE	LOOK
HE'D	WOULDN'T	BEFORE	I'VE	THEY'LL
I'M	WHAT'S	IT'S	THAT'S	YOU'RE
YOU	LEAP	WE'RE	HOW'S	CAN'T
DOESN'T	WE'LL	I'LL	WOULD'VE	THEY'RE
DON'T	I'D	DIDN'T	HADN'T	COULDN'T
YOU'LL	AREN'T	YOU'VE	SHE'S	WHO'S
WASN'T	HE'S	YOU'D	SHOULD'VE	COULD'VE
WHAT'LL	WON'T	THEY'D	*	*

Write the proverb you uncovered. _____

What does the proverb mean? _____

Write four complete sentences. Use a contraction in each sentence.

_____

_____

_____

_____

I Have, Who Has?: Language Arts • 5–6 © 2006 Creative Teaching Press

I have the **first card.**

Who has the contraction for *you would*?

I have the contraction **who's.**

Who has the contraction for *we will*?

I have the contraction **you'd.**

Who has the contraction for *have not*?

I have the contraction **we'll.**

Who has the contraction for *they will*?

I have the contraction **haven't.**

Who has the contraction for *who would*?

I have the contraction **they'll.**

Who has the contraction for *he would*?

I have the contraction **who'd.**

Who has the contraction for *should not*?

I have the contraction **he'd.**

Who has the contraction for *were not*?

I have the contraction **shouldn't.**

Who has the contraction for *who is*?

I have the contraction **weren't.**

Who has the contraction for *I would*?

Contractions 2

I have the contraction
I'd.

Who has the contraction for
they are?

I have the contraction
when's.

Who has the contraction for
has not?

I have the contraction
they're.

Who has the contraction for
it will?

I have the contraction
hasn't.

Who has the contraction for
let us?

I have the contraction
it'll.

Who has the contraction for
what will?

I have the contraction
let's.

Who has the contraction for
he is?

I have the contraction
what'll.

Who has the contraction for
they have?

I have the contraction
he's.

Who has the contraction for
is not?

I have the contraction
they've.

Who has the contraction for
when is?

I have the contraction
isn't.

Who has the contraction for
where is?

I Have, Who Has?: Language Arts • 5–6 © 2006 Creative Teaching Press

Contractions 2

I have the contraction
where's.

Who has the contraction for
we would?

I have the contraction
they'd.

Who has the contraction for
here is?

I have the contraction
we'd.

Who has the contraction for
had not?

I have the contraction
here's.

Who has the contraction for
we are?

I have the contraction
hadn't.

Who has the contraction for
are not?

I have the contraction
we're.

Who has the contraction for
could not?

I have the contraction
aren't.

Who has the contraction for
would not?

I have the contraction
couldn't.

Who has the contraction for
she would?

I have the contraction
wouldn't.

Who has the contraction for
they would?

I have the contraction
she'd.

Who has the contraction for
it is?

Contractions 2

I have the contraction
it's.

Who has the contraction for
there is?

I have the contraction
there's.

Who has the contraction for
do not?

I have the contraction
don't.

Who has the contraction for
will not?

I have the contraction
won't.

Who has the contraction for
that will?

I have the contraction
that'll.

Who has the contraction for
I will?

I have the contraction
I'll.

Who has the contraction for
she will?

I have the contraction
she'll.

Who has the contraction for
how is?

I have the contraction
how's.

Who has the contraction for
what is?

I have the contraction
what's.

Who has the contraction for
I am?

I have the contraction
I'm.

Who has the first card?

I Have, Who Has?: Language Arts • 5–6 © 2006 Creative Teaching Press

Contractions 2

As your classmates identify each contraction, lightly color in the matching box. Listen closely so you don't miss any answers. Read the words in the remaining boxes from top to bottom and left to right to uncover the hidden proverb.

IN	YOU'D	WHAT'S	SHOULDN'T	ONE
WHO'S	SHE'D	WOULDN'T	DON'T	HE'D
WEREN'T	EAR	THEY'D	AND OUT	I'D
WHO'D	WHAT'LL	I'LL	WHEN'S	THE
WHERE'S	I'M	LET'S	IT'S	ISN'T
WE'D	SHE'LL	HE'S	HOW'S	HADN'T
OTHER	HASN'T	THAT'LL	THEY'VE	HAVEN'T
IT'LL	THERE'S	HERE'S	WON'T	THEY'RE
WE'LL	COULDN'T	AREN'T	WE'RE	THEY'LL

Write the proverb you uncovered. _____

Write four complete sentences. Use a contraction in each sentence.

_____

_____

_____

_____

Contractions 3

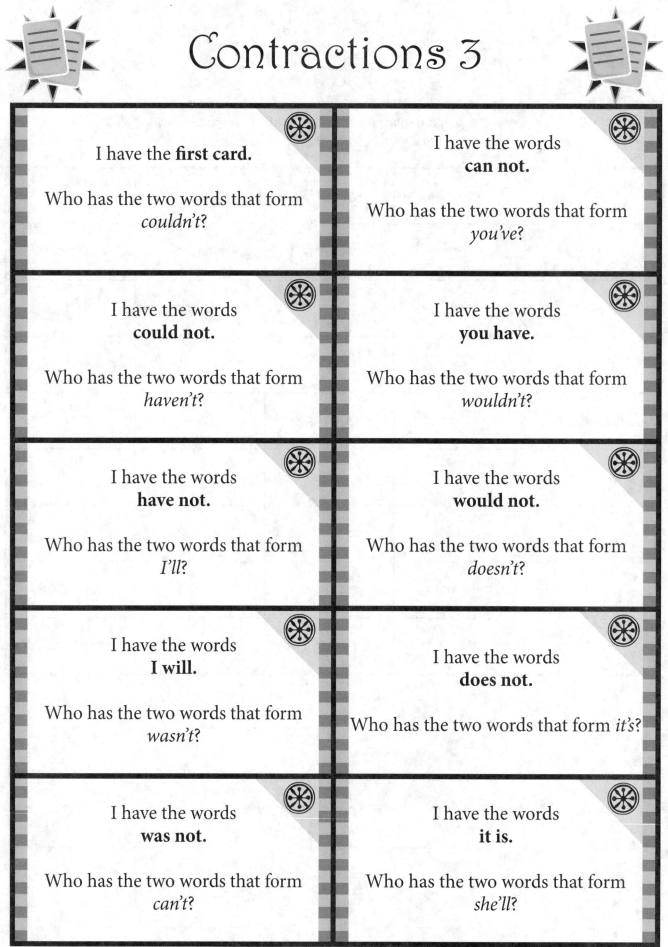

I have the **first card.**

Who has the two words that form *couldn't*?

I have the words **can not.**

Who has the two words that form *you've*?

I have the words **could not.**

Who has the two words that form *haven't*?

I have the words **you have.**

Who has the two words that form *wouldn't*?

I have the words **have not.**

Who has the two words that form *I'll*?

I have the words **would not.**

Who has the two words that form *doesn't*?

I have the words **I will.**

Who has the two words that form *wasn't*?

I have the words **does not.**

Who has the two words that form *it's*?

I have the words **was not.**

Who has the two words that form *can't*?

I have the words **it is.**

Who has the two words that form *she'll*?

I Have, Who Has?: Language Arts • 5–6 © 2006 Creative Teaching Press

Contractions 3

I have the words
she will.

Who has the two words that form
he'll?

I have the words
had not.

Who has the two words that form
we're?

I have the words
he will.

Who has the two words that form
who'll?

I have the words
we are.

Who has the two words that form
didn't?

I have the words
who will.

Who has the two words that form
isn't?

I have the words
did not.

Who has the two words that form
she's?

I have the words
is not.

Who has the two words that form
I'm?

I have the words
she is.

Who has the two words that form
she'd?

I have the words
I am.

Who has the two words that form
hadn't?

I have the words
she would.

Who has the two words that form
he's?

I Have, Who Has?: Language Arts • 5–6 © 2006 Creative Teaching Press

Contractions 3

I have the words
he is.

Who has the two words that form
hasn't?

I have the words
he would.

Who has the two words that form
they're?

I have the words
has not.

Who has the two words that form
let's?

I have the words
they are.

Who has the two words that form
aren't?

I have the words
let us.

Who has the two words that form
we've?

I have the words
are not.

Who has the two words that form
you're?

I have the words
we have.

Who has the two words that form
they've?

I have the words
you are.

Who has the two words that form
weren't?

I have the words
they have.

Who has the two words that form
he'd?

I have the words
were not.

Who has the two words that form
don't?

I Have, Who Has?: Language Arts • 5–6 © 2006 Creative Teaching Press

Contractions 3

I have the words
do not.

Who has the two words that form
I've?

I have the words
should not.

Who has the two words that form
won't?

I have the words
I have.

Who has the two words that form
they'll?

I have the words
will not.

Who has the two words that form
we'll?

I have the words
they will.

Who has the two words that form
could've?

I have the words
we will.

Who has the two words that form
it'll?

I have the words
could have.

Who has the two words that form
I'd?

I have the words
it will.

Who has the two words that form
you'll?

I have the words
I would.

Who has the two words that form
shouldn't?

I have the words
you will.

Who has the first card?

I Have, Who Has? Language Arts • 5–6 © 2006 Creative Teaching Press

Contractions 3

As your classmates identify each answer, lightly color in the matching box. Listen closely so you don't miss any answers. Read the words in the remaining boxes from top to bottom and left to right to uncover the hidden proverb.

SHE WOULD	ARE NOT	SHE IS	THEY WILL	WE HAVE
THERE	COULD NOT	IS NO	WOULD NOT	PLACE
HE WILL	LIKE	LET US	HOME	WAS NOT
IT WILL	THEY HAVE	I WOULD	YOU ARE	SHOULD NOT
CAN NOT	SHE WILL	WHO WILL	WE ARE	IS NOT
HAD NOT	DID NOT	WILL NOT	HAVE NOT	HE WOULD
IT IS	DO NOT	HE IS	I HAVE	DOES NOT
THEY ARE	WE WILL	HAS NOT	WERE NOT	I AM
COULD HAVE	I WILL	YOU WILL	YOU HAVE	*

Write the proverb you uncovered. _____

Write four complete sentences. Use a contraction in each sentence.

_____

_____

_____

_____

I Have, Who Has?: Language Arts • 5–6 © 2006 Creative Teaching Press

Details to the Main Idea 1

I have the **first card.**

Who has the category for radish, corn, asparagus?

I have **jewelry.**

Who has the category for slippers, socks, shoes?

I have **vegetables.**

Who has the category for ball, circle, tire?

I have **things worn on your feet.**

Who has the category for marker, colored pencil, crayon?

I have **things that are round.**

Who has the category for French, Chinese, Spanish?

I have **things used for drawing.**

Who has the category for truck, plane, jet?

I have **languages.**

Who has the category for green, aqua, purple?

I have **forms of transportation.**

Who has the category for trout, cod, salmon?

I have **colors.**

Who has the category for necklace, earrings, watch?

I have **fish.**

Who has the category for anchor, boulder, truck?

I have **heavy things.**

Who has the category for twelve, twenty, thirty-two?

I have **loud sounds.**

Who has the category for elm, oak, maple?

I have **even numbers.**

Who has the category for school bus, lemon, sun?

I have **trees.**

Who has the category for retriever, cocker spaniel, poodle?

I have **yellow things.**

Who has the category for South America, Asia, Africa?

I have **dogs.**

Who has the category for stormy, sunny, snowy?

I have **continents.**

Who has the category for square, triangle, rectangle?

I have **weather.**

Who has the category for tulip, rose, daffodil?

I have **linear shapes.**

Who has the category for siren, horn, scream?

I have **flowers.**

Who has the category for kangaroo, grasshopper, rabbit?

I Have, Who Has?: Language Arts • 5–6 © 2006 Creative Teaching Press

Details to the Main Idea 1

I have
animals that hop.

Who has the category for
November, May, August?

I have
U.S. presidents.

Who has the category for
arm, neck, leg?

I have
months.

Who has the category for
flashlight, sun, lamp?

I have
body parts.

Who has the category for
bus, taxi, train?

I have
things that give light.

Who has the category for
magazines, bills, letters?

I have
types of ground transportation.

Who has the category for
soda, coffee, hot cocoa?

I have
things that come in the mail.

Who has the category for
sister, uncle, grandma?

I have
beverages.

Who has the category for
stop sign, blood, strawberry?

I have
relatives.

Who has the category for
Roosevelt, Clinton, Bush?

I have
red things.

Who has the category for
breakfast, dinner, lunch?

I Have, Who Has? Language Arts • 5–6 © 2006 Creative Teaching Press

Details to the Main Idea 1

I have
meal times.

Who has the category for
leaf, grass, dollar bill?

I have
kitchen appliances.

Who has the category for
penny, dime, nickel?

I have
green things.

Who has the category for
strawberry, orange, plum?

I have
coins.

Who has the category for
France, Spain, England?

I have
fruit.

Who has the category for
golf, tennis, baseball?

I have
countries in Europe.

Who has the category for
rubber band, elastic, suspenders?

I have
sports.

Who has the category for
sherbert, ice, snow?

I have
things that stretch.

Who has the category for
goat, pig, cow?

I have
cold things.

Who has the category for
refrigerator, microwave, stove?

I have
farm animals.

Who has the first card?

I Have, Who Has?: Language Arts • 5–6 © 2006 Creative Teaching Press

Details to the Main Idea 1

As your classmates identify each category, lightly color in the matching box. Listen closely so you don't miss any answers. Read the words in the remaining boxes from top to bottom and left to right to uncover the hidden proverb.

THINGS USED FOR DRAWING	LOUD SOUNDS	EVEN NUMBERS	THINGS THAT COME IN THE MAIL	THINGS THAT ARE ROUND
COLD THINGS	VEGETABLES	THE GRASS	RED THINGS	IS ALWAYS
CONTINENTS	MONTHS	TYPES OF GROUND TRANSPORTATION	HEAVY THINGS	COUNTRIES IN EUROPE
SPORTS	FRUIT	YELLOW THINGS	TREES	RELATIVES
LANGUAGES	ANIMALS THAT HOP	GREENER	ON THE OTHER SIDE	THINGS WORN ON YOUR FEET
WEATHER	OF THE	BEVERAGES	DOGS	MEAL TIMES
FARM ANIMALS	FENCE	FISH	COINS	BODY PARTS
FORMS OF TRANSPORTATION	FLOWERS	GREEN THINGS	JEWELRY	THINGS THAT GIVE LIGHT
KITCHEN APPLIANCES	COLORS	U.S. PRESIDENTS	LINEAR SHAPES	THINGS THAT STRETCH

Write the proverb you uncovered. _____

Create four new categories of your own. List three items that would fit in each category.

_____

_____

_____

_____

I Have, Who Has?: Language Arts • 5–6 © 2006 Creative Teaching Press

Details to the Main Idea 2

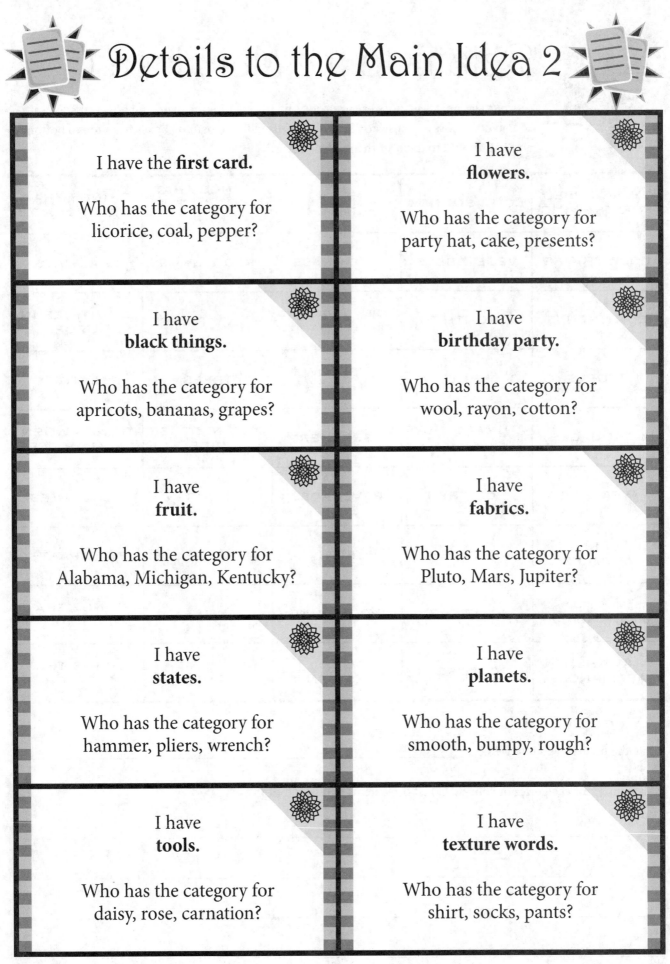

I have the **first card.**

Who has the category for licorice, coal, pepper?

I have **flowers.**

Who has the category for party hat, cake, presents?

I have **black things.**

Who has the category for apricots, bananas, grapes?

I have **birthday party.**

Who has the category for wool, rayon, cotton?

I have **fruit.**

Who has the category for Alabama, Michigan, Kentucky?

I have **fabrics.**

Who has the category for Pluto, Mars, Jupiter?

I have **states.**

Who has the category for hammer, pliers, wrench?

I have **planets.**

Who has the category for smooth, bumpy, rough?

I have **tools.**

Who has the category for daisy, rose, carnation?

I have **texture words.**

Who has the category for shirt, socks, pants?

I Have, Who Has?: Language Arts • 5–6 © 2006 Creative Teaching Press

Details to the Main Idea 2

I have **clothing.**

Who has the category for luau, hula, lei?

I have **cheeses.**

Who has the category for Latin, German, French?

I have **things from Hawaii.**

Who has the category for vanilla, strawberry, chocolate?

I have **languages.**

Who has the category for cashew, macadamia, walnut?

I have **ice-cream flavors.**

Who has the category for tables, food, waitress?

I have **nuts.**

Who has the category for spoon, milk, bowl?

I have **restaurant.**

Who has the category for peas, beans, broccoli?

I have **cereal.**

Who has the category for the Amazon, Nile, Rio Grande?

I have **vegetables.**

Who has the category for jack, cheddar, mozzarella?

I have **rivers.**

Who has the category for doorknob, wheel, dial?

Details to the Main Idea 2

I have
things that turn.

Who has the category for
mouth, eyes, nose?

I have
things on an airplane.

Who has the category for
glass, paper, plastic?

I have
face parts.

Who has the category for
sight, smell, touch?

I have
things to recycle.

Who has the category for
pigeon, crow, blue jay?

I have
senses.

Who has the category for
tambourine, piano, guitar?

I have
birds.

Who has the category for
knife, spoon, fork?

I have
musical instruments.

Who has the category for
sprinter, jet, cheetah?

I have
utensils.

Who has the category for
foggy, rainy, overcast?

I have
fast things.

Who has the category for
pilot, stewardess, luggage?

I have
weather forecast terms.

Who has the category for
kitchen, den, bedroom?

I Have, Who Has?: Language Arts • 5–6 © 2006 Creative Teaching Press

Details to the Main Idea 2

I have
rooms in a house.

Who has the category for
brakes, engine, transmission?

I have
meats.

Who has the category for
snap, pop, crunch?

I have
parts of a car.

Who has the category for the
Pacific, Atlantic, Indian?

I have
sound words.

Who has the category for
razor, scissors, knife?

I have
oceans.

Who has the category for
Los Angeles, Chicago, Philadelphia?

I have
things that cut.

Who has the category for
frustration, joy, sadness?

I have
major cities.

Who has the category for
jazz, blues, rock?

I have
feelings.

Who has the category for
bee, fly, mosquito?

I have
types of music.

Who has the category for
beef, turkey, pork?

I have
flying insects.

Who has the first card?

Details to the Main Idea 2

As your classmates identify each category, lightly color in the matching box. Listen closely so you don't miss any answers. Read the words in the remaining boxes from top to bottom and left to right to uncover the hidden proverb.

FLOWERS	ABSENCE	RIVERS	MAKES	FRUIT
THE	ICE-CREAM FLAVORS	FACE PARTS	THINGS THAT TURN	TYPES OF MUSIC
CEREAL	RESTAURANT	HEART	PLANETS	UTENSILS
THINGS THAT CUT	OCEANS	BIRDS	CLOTHING	SENSES
NUTS	LANGUAGES	FEELINGS	STATES	ROOMS IN A HOUSE
MAJOR CITIES	GROW	PARTS OF A CAR	VEGETABLES	CHEESES
THINGS TO RECYCLE	TEXTURE WORDS	MUSICAL INSTRUMENTS	FLYING INSECTS	MEATS
SOUND WORDS	FABRICS	WEATHER FORECAST TERMS	THINGS FROM HAWAII	FAST THINGS
BLACK THINGS	TOOLS	THINGS ON AN AIRPLANE	BIRTHDAY PARTY	FONDER

Write the proverb you uncovered. _____

Create four new categories of your own. List three items that would fit in each category.

_____

_____

_____

I Have, Who Has?: Language Arts • 5–6 © 2006 Creative Teaching Press

Main Idea to Details 1

I have the **first card.**

Who has continents?

I have
polka, square, tap.

Who has flowers?

I have
Africa, Europe, Asia.

Who has inflatable things?

I have
tulip, daisy, rose.

Who has rooms?

I have
tires, balloons, rubber balls.

Who has household appliances?

I have
living room, office, den.

Who has cats?

I have
blender, iron, coffeemaker.

Who has tools?

I have
jaguars, pumas, leopards.

Who has parts of speech?

I have
screwdriver, saw, hammer.

Who has dances?

I have
adjectives, verbs, conjunctions.

Who has vehicles?

I Have, Who Has?: Language Arts • 5–6 © 2006 Creative Teaching Press

Main Idea to Details 1

I have
limousine, truck, van.

Who has cold things?

I have
stamen, root, flower.

Who has games?

I have
soda, ice, Arctic.

Who has sports?

I have
checkers, chess, cards.

Who has forms of communication?

I have
tennis, golf, volleyball.

Who has things on a pizza?

I have
e-mail, letters, telephone calls.

Who has states?

I have
cheese, sausage, pepperoni.

Who has languages?

I have
Ohio, Idaho, Hawaii.

Who has bones?

I have
Latin, Farsi, Greek.

Who has parts of a plant?

I have
femur, tibia, fibula.

Who has things on a farm?

I Have, Who Has?: Language Arts • 5–6 © 2006 Creative Teaching Press

Main Idea to Details 1

I have
pigs, goats, tractor.

Who has birds?

I have
popcorn, soda, movie.

Who has office supplies?

I have
gulls, eagles, owls.

Who has body organs?

I have
stapler, paper clips, pen.

Who has three-dimensional shapes?

I have
liver, spleen, heart.

Who has countries?

I have
sphere, cone, pyramid.

Who has drinks?

I have
China, Brazil, Canada.

Who has odd numbers?

I have
coffee, tea, juice.

Who has meats?

I have
fifteen, nine, seven.

Who has things at a movie theater?

I have
turkey, pork, beef.

Who has emotions?

I Have, Who Has?: Language Arts • 5–6 © 2006 Creative Teaching Press

I have
angry, sad, happy.

Who has linear shapes?

I have
fall, summer, spring.

Who has chores?

I have
circle, hexagon, triangle.

Who has things found in a hospital?

I have
dusting, bedmaking, sweeping.

Who has things found at the beach?

I have
thermometer, bed, nurse.

Who has things found in a classroom?

I have **shells, towels, sand.**

Who has candy?

I have
desks, ruler, paper.

Who has musical instruments?

I have
lollipops, jawbreakers, licorice.

Who has things used for hair?

I have
trombone, flute, drums.

Who has seasons?

I have
brush, hair dryer, comb.

Who has the first card?

Main Idea to Details 1

As your classmates identify the details that match each main idea, lightly color in the matching box. Listen closely so you don't miss any answers.

CARROTS, ASPARAGUS, KALE	TURKEY, PORK, BEEF	JAGUARS, PUMAS, LEOPARDS	ADJECTIVES, VERBS, CONJUNCTIONS	BROCCOLI, CAULIFLOWER, CELERY
FALL, SUMMER, SPRING	AFRICA, EUROPE, ASIA	TENNIS, GOLF, VOLLEYBALL	ONIONS, ENDIVE, CORN	ANGRY, SAD, HAPPY
CHEESE, SAUSAGE, PEPPERONI	STAPLER, PAPER CLIPS, PEN	CIRCLE, HEXAGON, TRIANGLE	THERMOMETER, BED, NURSE	TIRES, BALLOONS, RUBBER BALLS
BLENDER, IRON, COFFEEMAKER	BRUSH, HAIR DRYER, COMB	LATIN, FARSI, GREEK	PIGS, GOATS, TRACTOR	COFFEE, TEA, JUICE
BEANS, PEAS, SPROUTS	GULLS, EAGLES, OWLS	LIVING ROOM, OFFICE, DEN	OHIO, IDAHO, HAWAII	SODA, ICE, ARCTIC
E-MAIL, LETTERS, TELEPHONE CALLS	DUSTING, BEDMAKING, SWEEPING	SHELLS, TOWELS, SAND	STAMEN, ROOT, FLOWER	POPCORN, SODA, MOVIE
LETTUCE, MUSHROOMS, CILANTRO	SCREWDRIVER, SAW, HAMMER	LIMOUSINE, TRUCK, VAN	FEMUR, TIBIA, FIBULA	FIFTEEN, NINE, SEVEN
LIVER, SPLEEN, HEART	SPINACH, RADISH, GINGER	SPHERE, CONE, PYRAMID	CHECKERS, CHESS, CARDS	POLKA, SQUARE, TAP
TROMBONE, FLUTE, DRUMS	TULIP, DAISY, ROSE	LOLLIPOPS, JAWBREAKERS, LICORICE	CHINA, BRAZIL, CANADA	DESKS, RULER, PAPER

What category could ALL of the leftover words fit into?

_____

List three more items that could be added to the same category.

_____

_____

Main Idea to Details 2

I have the **first card.**

Who has garbage?

I have
hares, kangaroos, grasshoppers.

Who has parts of a computer?

I have
old food, broken glass, rinds.

Who has salty snacks?

I have
mouse, keyboard, monitor.

Who has ways to buy things?

I have
pretzels, chips, crackers.

Who has things in a dishwasher?

I have
cash, check, charge.

Who has days of the week?

I have
dishes, glasses, plates.

Who has items on an address label?

I have
Tuesday, Friday, Monday.

Who has cardinal directions?

I have
zip code, name, state.

Who has animals that hop?

I have
east, north, west.

Who has soups?

I Have, Who Has?: Language Arts • 5–6 © 2006 Creative Teaching Press

Main Idea to Details 2

I have
vegetable, onion, chicken noodle.

Who has things that take practice?

I have
luggage, passport, tickets.

Who has things that are spicy?

I have
cursive writing, playing soccer, learning multiplication.

Who has things that grow?

I have
jalapeños, salsa, sauces.

Who has parts of the digestive system?

I have
plants, nails, hair.

Who has games?

I have
esophagus, intestine, mouth.

Who has animals?

I have
chess, hide-and-seek, tag.

Who has things at a dentist's office?

I have
chimps, bats, lemurs.

Who has things that are absorbent?

I have
filling, drill, toothbrush.

Who has things needed for travel?

I have
paper towels, sponges, washcloths.

Who has yellow things?

I Have, Who Has?: Language Arts • 5–6 © 2006 Creative Teaching Press

Main Idea to Details 2

I have
the sun, school bus, lemon.

Who has things that float?

I have
papers, fingernails, bills.

Who has things at a clothing store?

I have
canoes, surfboards, logs.

Who has things used
in construction?

I have
cash register, pants, clerks.

Who has things at a bank?

I have
tractors, bulldozers, wood.

Who has gooey items?

I have
tellers, vault, money.

Who has types of muffins?

I have
**slime, mud, melted
marshmallows.**

Who has things that use batteries?

I have
chocolate, bran, corn.

Who has states?

I have
camera, remote control, radio.

Who has things that are filed?

I have
Missouri, Montana, Louisiana.

Who has things that bite?

I Have, Who Has?: Language Arts • 5–6 © 2006 Creative Teaching Press

Main Idea to Details 2

I have
bug, snake, mosquito.

Who has things that are green?

I have
October, May, March.

Who has beverages?

I have
limes, asparagus, broccoli.

Who has things in a salad?

I have
tea, juice, water.

Who has things at a baseball game?

I have
croutons, carrots, lettuce.

Who has things at a gym?

I have
pitcher, umpire, fans.

Who has parts of the
respiratory system?

I have
weights, bars, towels.

Who has things used to write?

I have
lungs, trachea, nose.

Who has things that are noisy?

I have
pens, pencils, markers.

Who has months?

I have
machinery, concerts, static.

Who has the first card?

I Have, Who Has? Language Arts • 5-6 © 2006 Creative Teaching Press

Main Idea to Details 2

As your classmates identify the words that fit each category, lightly color in the matching box. Listen closely so you don't miss any answers.

MOUSE, KEYBOARD, MONITOR	LIMES, ASPARAGUS, BROCCOLI	OCTOBER, MAY, MARCH	PAPER TOWELS, SPONGES, WASHCLOTHS	TEA, JUICE, WATER
TRACTORS, BULLDOZERS, WOOD	EAGLE, WOODPECKER, GULL	OLD FOOD, BROKEN GLASS, RINDS	CROUTONS, CARROTS, LETTUCE	BUG, SNAKE, MOSQUITO
SLIME, MUD, MELTED MARSHMALLOWS	HARES, KANGAROOS, GRASSHOPPERS	CHESS, HIDE-AND-SEEK, TAG	CURSIVE WRITING, PLAYING SOCCER, LEARNING MULTIPLICATION	PRETZELS, CHIPS, CRACKERS
PLANTS, NAILS, HAIR	KESTREL, ROBIN, PELICAN	ESOPHAGUS, INTESTINE, MOUTH	PITCHER, UMPIRE, FANS	PENS, PENCILS, MARKERS
CASH REGISTER, PANTS, CLERKS	CANOES, SURFBOARDS, LOGS	LUNGS, TRACHEA, NOSE	TELLERS, VAULT, MONEY	CHIMPS, BATS, LEMURS
SWALLOW, ORIOLE, PARROT	DISHES, GLASSES, PLATES	JALAPEÑOS, SALSA, SAUCES	FILLING, DRILL, TOOTHBRUSH	CAMERA, REMOTE CONTROL, RADIO
EAST, NORTH, WEST	HAWK, PIGEON, DOVE	CHOCOLATE, BRAN, CORN	ZIP CODE, NAME, STATE	CASH, CHECK, CHARGE
PENGUIN, HERON, WARBLER	TUESDAY, FRIDAY, MONDAY	WEIGHTS, BARS, TOWELS	VEGETABLE, ONION, CHICKEN NOODLE	PAPERS, FINGERNAILS, BILLS
LUGGAGE, PASSPORT, TICKETS	THE SUN, SCHOOL BUS, LEMON	PHEASANT, OWL, DUCK	MISSOURI, MONTANA, LOUISIANA	MACHINERY, CONCERTS, STATIC

What category could ALL the leftover words fit into? _____

List three more items that could be added to the same category.

_____

_____

_____

I Have, Who Has?: Language Arts • 5–6 © 2006 Creative Teaching Press

Details to Main Idea to Details 1

I have the **first card.**

Who has a word that fits the same category as *German, French,* and *English*?

I have **touchdown.**

Who has a word that fits the same category as *toothbrush, thumb,* and *retainer*?

I have **Russian.**

Who has a word that fits the same category as *tiger, elephant,* and *cheetah*?

I have **fork.**

Who has a word that fits the same category as *hut, house,* and *mansion*?

I have **monkey.**

Who has a word that fits the same category as *squash, beets,* and *cauliflower*?

I have **tent.**

Who has a word that fits the same category as *vanilla, chocolate,* and *strawberry*?

I have **broccoli.**

Who has a word that fits the same category as *blueberry, apple,* and *peach*?

I have **caramel.**

Who has a word that fits the same category as *tuxedo, penguin,* and *newspaper*?

I have **watermelon.**

Who has a word that fits the same category as *hike, pass,* and *quarterback*?

I have **piano keys.**

Who has a word that fits the same category as *wrench, pliers,* and *screwdriver*?

I Have, Who Has? Language Arts • 5–6 © 2006 Creative Teaching Press

I have **hammer.**

Who has a word that fits the same category as *dogs, rabbits,* and *hamsters*?

I have **jelly beans.**

Who has a word that fits the same category as *grass, lettuce,* and *cucumber*?

I have **cats.**

Who has a word that fits the same category as *March, July,* and *November*?

I have **leaves.**

Who has a word that fits the same category as *chair, stool,* and *couch*?

I have **April.**

Who has a word that fits the same category as *towel, bucket,* and *bathing suit*?

I have **sofa.**

Who has a word that fits the same category as *eye shadow, mascara,* and *powder*?

I have **suntan lotion.**

Who has a word that fits the same category as *cousin, aunt,* and *mother*?

I have **lipstick.**

Who has a word that fits the same category as *coral reef, fish,* and *submarine*?

I have **grandmother.**

Who has a word that fits the same category as *gumdrops, taffy,* and *candy corn*?

I have **diver.**

Who has a word that fits the same category as *simmer, bake,* and *boil*?

I Have, Who Has?: Language Arts • 5–6 © 2006 Creative Teaching Press

I have **fry.**

Who has a word that fits the same category as *magenta, lilac,* and *aqua*?

I have **oven.**

Who has a word that fits the same category as *spelling, writing,* and *geography*?

I have **fuchsia.**

Who has a word that fits the same category as *femur, tibia,* and *patella*?

I have **science.**

Who has a word that fits the same category as *Old Maid, Hearts,* and *Go Fish*?

I have **fibula.**

Who has a word that fits the same category as *baseball, soccer,* and *volleyball*?

I have **Solitaire.**

Who has a word that fits the same category as *snowmobile, sled,* and *toboggan*?

I have **basketball.**

Who has a word that fits the same category as *emerald, ruby,* and *diamond*?

I have **skis.**

Who has a word that fits the same category as *tornado, tsunami,* and *hurricane*?

I have **sapphire.**

Who has a word that fits the same category as *stove, sink,* and *refrigerator*?

I have **typhoon.**

Who has a word that fits the same category as *keyboard, mouse,* and *monitor*?

I have **CD-Rom drive.**

Who has a word that fits the same category as *teddy bear, bike,* and *doll*?

I have **ostrich.**

Who has a word that fits the same category as *chess, cards,* and *backgammon*?

I have **yo-yo.**

Who has a word that fits the same category as *winter, fall,* and *spring*?

I have **checkers.**

Who has a word that fits the same category as *thirty, seventy,* and *twenty*?

I have **summer.**

Who has a word that fits the same category as *coin purse, wallet,* and *bank vault*?

I have **fifty.**

Who has a word that fits the same category as *oyster, shrimp,* and *clam*?

I have **piggy bank.**

Who has a word that fits the same category as *headband, earrings,* and *glasses*?

I have **scallop.**

Who has a word that fits the same category as *carnation, tulip,* and *rose*?

I have **hat.**

Who has a word that fits the same category as *finch, parrot,* and *blue jay*?

I have **daisy.**

Who has the first card?

I Have, Who Has?: Language Arts • 5–6 © 2006 Creative Teaching Press

Details to Main Idea to Details 1

As your classmates identify each detail that fits the main idea, lightly color in the matching box. Listen closely so you don't miss any answers.

RUSSIAN	CATS	BUS	CARAMEL	BASKETBALL
SUMMER	SOLITAIRE	JELLY BEANS	HAT	AIRPLANE
APRIL	DAISY	TENT	DIVER	FIBULA
FUCHSIA	TRUCK	FRY	YO-YO	MONKEY
FORK	PIGGY BANK	TRAIN	SCIENCE	SCALLOP
SUNTAN LOTION	SKIS	LEAVES	PIANO KEYS	GRANDMOTHER
JET	CHECKERS	SOFA	LIPSTICK	SUBWAY
OVEN	HAMMER	OSTRICH	TYPHOON	BROCCOLI
TOUCHDOWN	SAPPHIRE	CD-ROM DRIVE	WATERMELON	FIFTY

What category could ALL the leftover words fit into? _____

List three more items that could be added to the same category.

_____

_____

_____

I Have, Who Has?: Language Arts • 5–6 © 2006 Creative Teaching Press

I have the **first card.**

Who has a word that fits the same category as *Europe, Asia,* and *Antarctica*?

I have **hexagon.**

Who has a word that fits the same category as *fall, summer,* and *spring*?

I have **North America.**

Who has a word that fits the same category as *chocolate chip, oatmeal,* and *peanut butter*?

I have **winter.**

Who has a word that fits the same category as *taste buds, teeth,* and *gums*?

I have **snickerdoodles.**

Who has a word that fits the same category as *tea, water,* and *juice*?

I have **tongue.**

Who has a word that fits the same category as *cereal, toast,* and *waffles*?

I have **soda.**

Who has a word that fits the same category as *owls, bats,* and *raccoons*?

I have **pancakes.**

Who has a word that fits the same category as *Cheddar, Monterey Jack,* and *Parmesan*?

I have **opossums.**

Who has a word that fits the same category as *octagon, nonagon,* and *pentagon*?

I have **Swiss.**

Who has a word that fits the same category as *sourdough, wheat,* and *pumpernickel*?

I Have, Who Has?: Language Arts • 5–6 © 2006 Creative Teaching Press

Details to Main Idea to Details 2

I have **rye.**

Who has a word that fits the same category as *happy, sorrowful,* and *ecstatic*?

I have **planes.**

Who has a word that fits the same category as *verbs, adverbs,* and *conjunctions*?

I have **disappointed.**

Who has a word that fits the same category as *heart, liver,* and *lungs*?

I have **adjectives.**

Who has a word that fits the same category as *Friday, Monday,* and *Saturday*?

I have **kidney.**

Who has a word that fits the same category as *lantern, canteen,* and *sleeping bag*?

I have **Tuesday.**

Who has a word that fits the same category as *desks, books,* and *students*?

I have **tent.**

Who has a word that fits the same category as *dress, shorts,* and *socks*?

I have **teacher.**

Who has a word that fits the same category as *turtle, aardvark,* and *snail*?

I have **sweater.**

Who has a word that fits the same category as *cars, boats,* and *trains*?

I have **hermit crab.**

Who has a word that fits the same category as *sausage, pepperoni,* and *pineapple*?

I Have, Who Has?: Language Arts • 5–6 © 2006 Creative Teaching Press

Details to Main Idea to Details 2

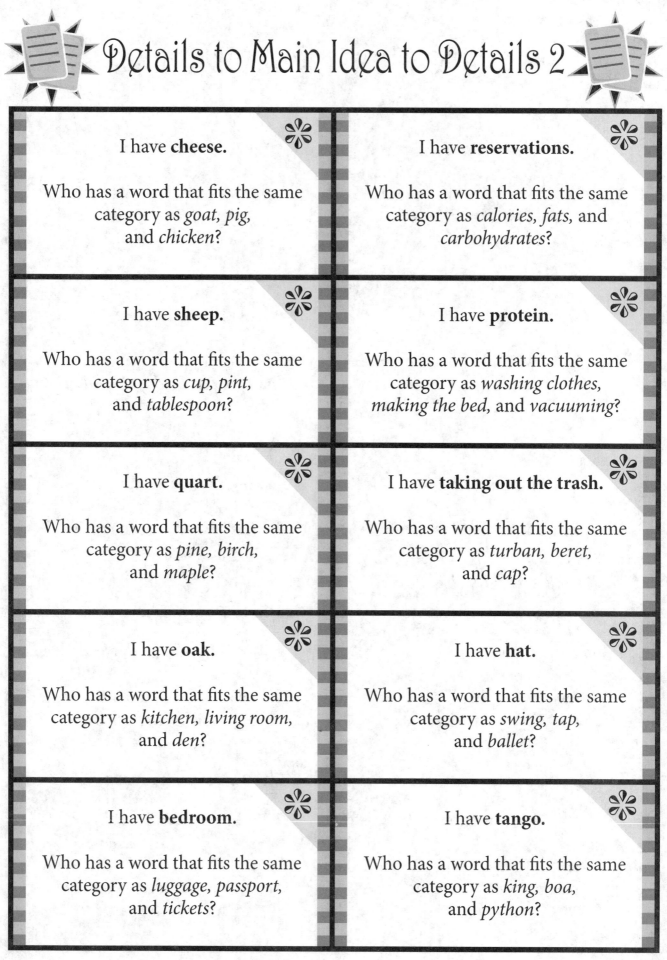

I have **cheese.**

Who has a word that fits the same category as *goat, pig,* and *chicken*?

I have **reservations.**

Who has a word that fits the same category as *calories, fats,* and *carbohydrates*?

I have **sheep.**

Who has a word that fits the same category as *cup, pint,* and *tablespoon*?

I have **protein.**

Who has a word that fits the same category as *washing clothes, making the bed,* and *vacuuming*?

I have **quart.**

Who has a word that fits the same category as *pine, birch,* and *maple*?

I have **taking out the trash.**

Who has a word that fits the same category as *turban, beret,* and *cap*?

I have **oak.**

Who has a word that fits the same category as *kitchen, living room,* and *den*?

I have **hat.**

Who has a word that fits the same category as *swing, tap,* and *ballet*?

I have **bedroom.**

Who has a word that fits the same category as *luggage, passport,* and *tickets*?

I have **tango.**

Who has a word that fits the same category as *king, boa,* and *python*?

I Have, Who Has?: Language Arts • 5–6 © 2006 Creative Teaching Press

I have **rattlesnake.**

Who has a word that fits the same category as *aluminum, steel,* and *copper*?

I have **"Exit."**

Who has a word that fits the same category as *root, stamen,* and *leaves*?

I have **titanium.**

Who has a word that fits the same category as *croutons, lettuce,* and *cheese*?

I have **stem.**

Who has a word that fits the same category as *friends, pals,* and *chums*?

I have **salad dressing.**

Who has a word that fits the same category as *Dalmatian, Akita,* and *golden retriever*?

I have **buddies.**

Who has a word that fits the same category as *minestrone, vegetable,* and *chicken noodle*?

I have **poodle.**

Who has a word that fits the same category as *banana, mango,* and *grapefruit*?

I have **clam chowder.**

Who has a word that fits the same category as *baking soda, sugar,* and *cornstarch*?

I have **peach.**

Who has a word that fits the same category as *"Do not enter," "Yield,"* and *"Stop"*?

I have **flour.**

Who has the first card?

I Have, Who Has?: Language Arts • 5–6 © 2006 Creative Teaching Press

Details to Main Idea to Details 2

As your classmates identify each detail that fits the main idea, lightly color in the matching box. Listen closely so you don't miss any answers.

TONGUE	NORTH AMERICA	SWIM	PANCAKES	QUART
TUESDAY	JUMP	ADJECTIVES	"EXIT"	TEACHER
WINTER	SHEEP	TANGO	FLOUR	SWISS
PLANES	READ	PEACH	CHEESE	TITANIUM
BUDDIES	SWEATER	RATTLESNAKE	SNICKERDOODLES	RYE
HEXAGON	HAT	SALAD DRESSING	BUILD	BEDROOM
RUN	POODLE	HERMIT CRAB	TENT	RESERVATIONS
RIDE	STEM	OAK	PROTEIN	CLAM CHOWDER
OPOSSUMS	KIDNEY	TAKING OUT THE TRASH	SODA	DISAPPOINTED

What category could ALL the leftover words fit into? _____

List three more items that could be added to the same category.

_____

_____

_____

I Have, Who Has?: Language Arts • 5–6 © 2006 Creative Teaching Press

Plural Nouns

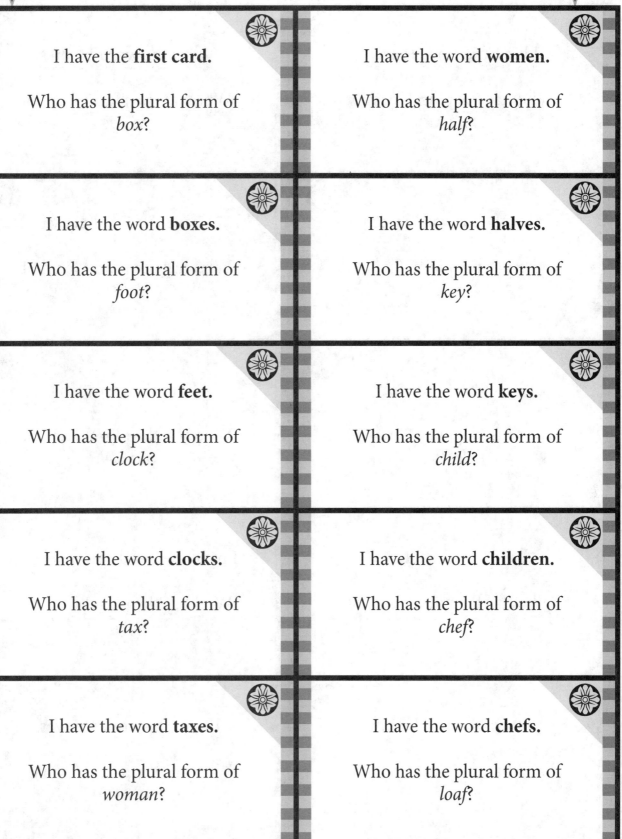

I have the **first card.**

Who has the plural form of
box?

I have the word **women.**

Who has the plural form of
half?

I have the word **boxes.**

Who has the plural form of
foot?

I have the word **halves.**

Who has the plural form of
key?

I have the word **feet.**

Who has the plural form of
clock?

I have the word **keys.**

Who has the plural form of
child?

I have the word **clocks.**

Who has the plural form of
tax?

I have the word **children.**

Who has the plural form of
chef?

I have the word **taxes.**

Who has the plural form of
woman?

I have the word **chefs.**

Who has the plural form of
loaf?

I Have, Who Has?: Language Arts • 5–6 © 2006 Creative Teaching Press

Plural Nouns

I have the word **loaves.**

Who has the plural form of *mouse?*

I have the word **bushes.**

Who has the plural form of *goose?*

I have the word **mice.**

Who has the plural form of *ring?*

I have the word **geese.**

Who has the plural form of *lab?*

I have the word **rings.**

Who has the plural form of *leaf?*

I have the word **labs.**

Who has the plural form of *sandwich?*

I have the word **leaves.**

Who has the plural form of *man?*

I have the word **sandwiches.**

Who has the plural form of *thief?*

I have the word **men.**

Who has the plural form of *bush?*

I have the word **thieves.**

Who has the plural form of *moose?*

I Have, Who Has?: Language Arts • 5–6 © 2006 Creative Teaching Press

Plural Nouns

I have the word **moose.**

Who has the plural form of
bus?

I have the word **teeth.**

Who has the plural form of
bunny?

I have the word **buses.**

Who has the plural form of
shelf?

I have the word **bunnies.**

Who has the plural form of
watch?

I have the word **shelves.**

Who has the plural form of
lunch?

I have the word **watches.**

Who has the plural form of
wish?

I have the word **lunches.**

Who has the plural form of
deer?

I have the word **wishes.**

Who has the plural form of
match?

I have the word **deer.**

Who has the plural form of
tooth?

I have the word **matches.**

Who has the plural form of
owl?

I Have, Who Has?: Language Arts • 5–6 © 2006 Creative Teaching Press

Plural Nouns

I have the word **owls.**

Who has the plural form of *fish*?

I have the word **kisses.**

Who has the plural form of *life*?

I have the word **fish.**

Who has the plural form of *ox*?

I have the word **lives.**

Who has the plural form of *sheep*?

I have the word **oxen.**

Who has the plural form of *cup*?

I have the word **sheep.**

Who has the plural form of *sky*?

I have the word **cups.**

Who has the plural form of *wife*?

I have the word **skies.**

Who has the plural form of *calf*?

I have the word **wives.**

Who has the plural form of *kiss*?

I have the word **calves.**

Who has the first card?

I Have, Who Has?: Language Arts • 5–6 © 2006 Creative Teaching Press

Plural Nouns

As your classmates identify each plural noun, lightly color in the matching box to uncover the hidden riddle and its answer. Listen closely so you don't miss any answers.

CHILDREN	THIEVES	CHEFS	SANDWICHES	BOXES
MICE	MATCHES	DEER	WISHES	LOAVES
WHAT	SHEEP	TEETH	LIVES	LABS
KEYS	DID	BUNNIES	THE	CHEWING
RINGS	SKIES	WATCHES	CALVES	GEESE
GUM	SAY TO	LUNCHES	THE	FEET
HALVES	SHOE	SHELVES	I'M	LEAVES
STUCK	WIVES	BUSES	KISSES	ON YOU
MEN	CUPS	MOOSE	OXEN	BUSHES
WOMEN	OWLS	TAXES	FISH	CLOCKS

Write the riddle and answer you uncovered.

_____

Write three complete sentences. Use at least one of the plural nouns listed above in each sentence.

_____

_____

I Have, Who Has?: Language Arts • 5–6 © 2006 Creative Teaching Press

Changing Present- to Past-Tense Verbs 1

I have the **first card.**

Who has the past-tense form of *sell*?

I have the word **bit.**

Who has the past-tense form of *pay*?

I have the word **sold.**

Who has the past-tense form of *eat*?

I have the word **paid.**

Who has the past-tense form of *fly*?

I have the word **ate.**

Who has the past-tense form of *blow*?

I have the word **flew.**

Who has the past-tense form of *give*?

I have the word **blew.**

Who has the past-tense form of *feed*?

I have the word **gave.**

Who has the past-tense form of *lead*?

I have the word **fed.**

Who has the past-tense form of *bite*?

I have the word **led.**

Who has the past-tense form of *bend*?

I Have, Who Has?: Language Arts • 5–6 © 2006 Creative Teaching Press

I have the word **bent.**

Who has the past-tense form of *throw*?

I have the word **drank.**

Who has the past-tense form of *say*?

I have the word **threw.**

Who has the past-tense form of *shake*?

I have the word **said.**

Who has the past-tense form of *write*?

I have the word **shook.**

Who has the past-tense form of *light*?

I have the word **wrote.**

Who has the past-tense form of *grow*?

I have the word **lit.**

Who has the past-tense form of *tell*?

I have the word **grew.**

Who has the past-tense form of *sing*?

I have the word **told.**

Who has the past-tense form of *drink*?

I have the word **sang.**

Who has the past-tense form of *wear*?

Changing Present- to Past-Tense Verbs 1

I have the word **wore.**

Who has the past-tense form of *take*?

I have the word **forgave.**

Who has the past-tense form of *know*?

I have the word **took.**

Who has the past-tense form of *make*?

I have the word **knew.**

Who has the past-tense form of *cling*?

I have the word **made.**

Who has the past-tense form of *sink*?

I have the word **clung.**

Who has the past-tense form of *catch*?

I have the word **sank.**

Who has the past-tense form of *teach*?

I have the word **caught.**

Who has the past-tense form of *hang*?

I have the word **taught.**

Who has the past-tense form of *forgive*?

I have the word **hung.**

Who has the past-tense form of *tear*?

I Have, Who Has?: Language Arts • 5–6 © 2006 Creative Teaching Press

Changing Present- to Past-Tense Verbs 1

I have the word **tore.**

Who has the past-tense form of *build*?

I have the word **cried.**

Who has the past-tense form of *lend*?

I have the word **built.**

Who has the past-tense form of *draw*?

I have the word **lent.**

Who has the past-tense form of *spend*?

I have the word **drew.**

Who has the past-tense form of *send*?

I have the word **spent.**

Who has the past-tense form of *run*?

I have the word **sent.**

Who has the past-tense form of *ring*?

I have the word **ran.**

Who has the past-tense form of *bring*?

I have the word **rang.**

Who has the past-tense form of *cry*?

I have the word **brought.**

Who has the first card?

Changing Present- to Past-Tense Verbs 1

As your classmates identify each past-tense verb, lightly color in the matching box to uncover the hidden riddle and its answer. Listen closely so you don't miss any answers.

FLEW	SANK	SENT	WHAT'S	TAUGHT
THREW	BLACK	SOLD	DRANK	AND
WHITE	TOLD	TORE	BUILT	PAID
BROUGHT	AND	BENT	SAID	DREW
ATE	LIT	PINK	SHOOK	SANG
ALL	HUNG	RAN	OVER	FORGAVE
GREW	CRIED	LED	AN	BIT
TOOK	BLEW	CAUGHT	KNEW	WORE
GAVE	EMBARRASSED	WROTE	FED	SPENT
LENT	MADE	ZEBRA	RANG	CLUNG

Write the riddle and answer you uncovered.

_____

Write three complete sentences. Use at least one of the past-tense verbs listed above in each sentence.

_____

_____

_____

I Have, Who Has?: Language Arts • 5–6 © 2006 Creative Teaching Press

I have the **first card.**

Who has the past-tense form of *lose?*

I have the word **froze.**

Who has the past-tense form of *sleep?*

I have the word **lost.**

Who has the past-tense form of *grow?*

I have the word **slept.**

Who has the past-tense form of *go?*

I have the word **grew.**

Who has the past-tense form of *wake?*

I have the word **went.**

Who has the past-tense form of *speak?*

I have the word **woke.**

Who has the past-tense form of *know?*

I have the word **spoke.**

Who has the past-tense form of *dive?*

I have the word **knew.**

Who has the past-tense form of *freeze?*

I have the word **dove.**

Who has the past-tense form of *find?*

Changing Present- to Past-Tense Verbs 2

I have the word **found**.

Who has the past-tense form of *choose*?

I have the word **called**.

Who has the past-tense form of *drive*?

I have the word **chose**.

Who has the past-tense form of *ring*?

I have the word **drove**.

Who has the past-tense form of *smash*?

I have the word **rang**.

Who has the past-tense form of *ride*?

I have the word **smashed**.

Who has the past-tense form of *creep*?

I have the word **rode**.

Who has the past-tense form of *charge*?

I have the word **crept**.

Who has the past-tense form of *write*?

I have the word **charged**.

Who has the past-tense form of *call*?

I have the word **wrote**.

Who has the past-tense form of *speed*?

I Have, Who Has?: Language Arts • 5–6 © 2006 Creative Teaching Press

I have the word **sped.**

Who has the past-tense form of *buy*?

I have the word **kept.**

Who has the past-tense form of *bleed*?

I have the word **bought.**

Who has the past-tense form of *hold*?

I have the word **bled.**

Who has the past-tense form of *fight*?

I have the word **held.**

Who has the past-tense form of *sweep*?

I have the word **fought.**

Who has the past-tense form of *get*?

I have the word **swept.**

Who has the past-tense form of *break*?

I have the word **got.**

Who has the past-tense form of *think*?

I have the word **broke.**

Who has the past-tense form of *keep*?

I have the word **thought.**

Who has the past-tense form of *lead*?

Changing Present- to Past-Tense Verbs 2

I have the word **led.**

Who has past-tense form of *meet*?

I have the word **lay.**

Who has the past-tense form of *laugh*?

I have the word **met.**

Who has the past-tense form of *weep*?

I have the word **laughed.**

Who has the past-tense form of *do*?

I have the word **wept.**

Who has the past-tense form of *file*?

I have the word **did.**

Who has the past-tense form of *eat*?

I have the word **filed.**

Who has the past-tense form of *sing*?

I have the word **ate.**

Who has the past-tense form of *blow*?

I have the word **sang.**

Who has the past-tense form of *lie*?

I have the word **blew.**

Who has the first card?

I Have, Who Has?: Language Arts • 5–6 © 2006 Creative Teaching Press

Changing Present- to Past-Tense Verbs 2

As your classmates identify each past-tense verb, lightly color in the matching box to uncover the hidden riddle and its answer. Listen closely so you don't miss any answers.

WEPT	BOUGHT	FOUND	MET	LOST
HELD	DID	WHY	WROTE	LAY
DO	DROVE	CHOSE	SWEPT	BIRDS
DOVE	FOUGHT	FLY	LED	GREW
SPOKE	FILED	RODE	ATE	SPED
THOUGHT	CALLED	SOUTH	CHARGED	BECAUSE
IT'S	GOT	RANG	TOO	BLED
WENT	BLEW	LAUGHED	CREPT	WOKE
FAR	SMASHED	BROKE	TO	KEPT
SLEPT	WALK	FROZE	SANG	KNEW

Write the riddle and answer you uncovered.

_____

Write three complete sentences. Use at least one of the past-tense verbs listed above in each sentence.

_____

_____

_____

Comparative and Superlative Adjectives

I have the **first card**.

Who has the comparative form of the adjective *bright*?

I have the word **shinier**.

Who has the superlative form of the adjective *furry*?

I have the word **brighter**.

Who has the superlative form of the adjective *big*?

I have the word **furriest**.

Who has the comparative form of the adjective *messy*?

I have the word **biggest**.

Who has the superlative form of the adjective *heavy*?

I have the word **messier**.

Who has the comparative form of the adjective *smart*?

I have the word **heaviest**.

Who has the comparative form of the adjective *nice*?

I have the word **smarter**.

Who has the superlative form of the adjective *fast*?

I have the word **nicer**.

Who has the comparative form of the adjective *shiny*?

I have the word **fastest**.

Who has the comparative form of the adjective *short*?

I Have, Who Has?: Language Arts • 5–6 © 2006 Creative Teaching Press

Comparative and Superlative Adjectives

I have the word **shorter**.

Who has the superlative form
of the adjective *thin*?

I have the word **faster**.

Who has the superlative form
of the adjective *shiny*?

I have the word **thinnest**.

Who has the superlative form
of the adjective *wise*?

I have the word **shiniest**.

Who has the superlative form
of the adjective *bright*?

I have the word **wisest**.

Who has the superlative form
of the adjective *smart*?

I have the word **brightest**.

Who has the superlative form
of the adjective *pretty*?

I have the word **smartest**.

Who has the comparative form
of the adjective *cheap*?

I have the word **prettiest**.

Who has the superlative form
of the adjective *nice*?

I have the word **cheaper**.

Who has the comparative form
of the adjective *fast*?

I have the word **nicest**.

Who has the superlative form
of the adjective *dirty*?

Comparative and Superlative Adjectives

I have the word **dirtiest.**

Who has the superlative form of the adjective *neat*?

I have the word **dirtier.**

Who has the comparative form of the adjective *cute*?

I have the word **neatest.**

Who has the superlative form of the adjective *messy*?

I have the word **cuter.**

Who has the superlative form of the adjective *tall*?

I have the word **messiest.**

Who has the comparative form of the adjective *mean*?

I have the word **tallest.**

Who has the comparative form of the adjective *heavy*?

I have the word **meaner.**

Who has the comparative form of the adjective *pretty*?

I have the word **heavier.**

Who has the superlative form of the adjective *mean*?

I have the word **prettier.**

Who has the comparative form of the adjective *dirty*?

I have the word **meanest.**

Who has the superlative form of the adjective *kind*?

I Have, Who Has?: Language Arts • 5–6 © 2006 Creative Teaching Press

Comparative and Superlative Adjectives

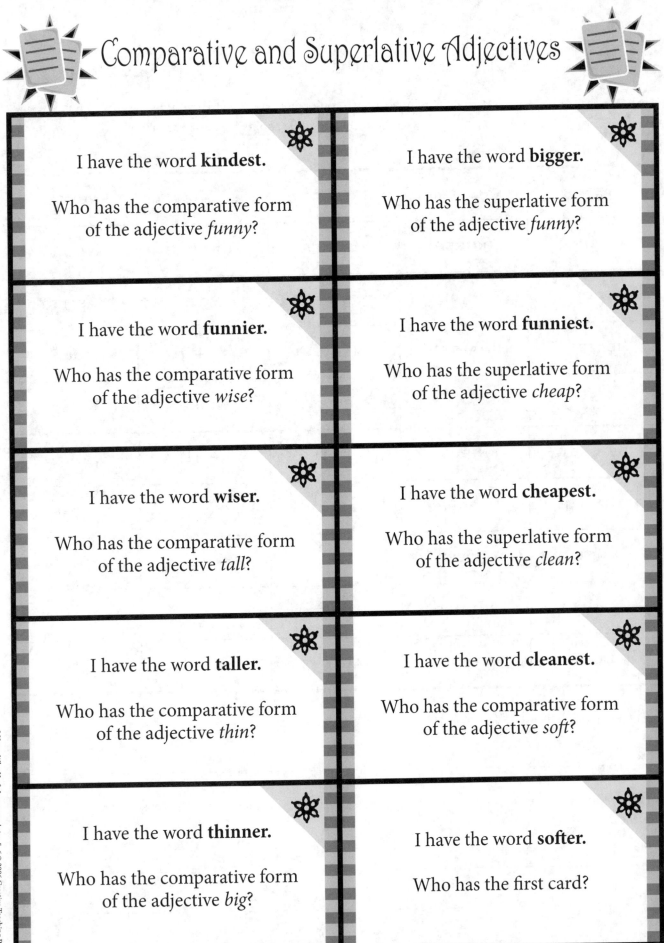

I have the word **kindest.**

Who has the comparative form of the adjective *funny*?

I have the word **bigger.**

Who has the superlative form of the adjective *funny*?

I have the word **funnier.**

Who has the comparative form of the adjective *wise*?

I have the word **funniest.**

Who has the superlative form of the adjective *cheap*?

I have the word **wiser.**

Who has the comparative form of the adjective *tall*?

I have the word **cheapest.**

Who has the superlative form of the adjective *clean*?

I have the word **taller.**

Who has the comparative form of the adjective *thin*?

I have the word **cleanest.**

Who has the comparative form of the adjective *soft*?

I have the word **thinner.**

Who has the comparative form of the adjective *big*?

I have the word **softer.**

Who has the first card?

I Have, Who Has?: Language Arts • 5–6 © 2006 Creative Teaching Press

Comparative and Superlative Adjectives

As your classmates identify each comparative and superlative adjective, lightly color in the matching box to uncover the hidden riddle and its answer. Listen closely so you don't miss any answers.

FASTER	CHEAPER	BRIGHTER	SHINIEST	PRETTIER
MESSIEST	BIGGER	MEANER	FURRIEST	WHAT
DO	FUNNIER	FUNNIEST	YOU	FASTEST
NEATEST	SMARTER	SMARTEST	BRIGHTEST	CALL
A	SCARED	DIRTIEST	WISER	NICER
BIGGEST	KINDEST	SHORTER	DIRTIER	DINOSAUR
THINNER	MESSIER	TALLER	CHEAPEST	PRETTIEST
THINNEST	NICEST	WISEST	HEAVIEST	SOFTER
MEANEST	SHINIER	CLEANEST	A	CUTER
HEAVIER	NERVOUS	TALLEST	REX	*

Write the riddle and answer you uncovered.

_____

Write three complete sentences. Use at least one of the comparative or superlative adjectives listed above in each sentence.

_____

_____

I Have, Who Has?: Language Arts • 5–6 © 2006 Creative Teaching Press

Nouns, Verbs, and Adjectives

I have the **first card.**

Who has the noun in
"The bulldozer is loud"?

I have the word **tired.**

Who has the noun in
"Your dog is gorgeous"?

I have the word **bulldozer.**

Who has the verb in
"Please call your mom"?

I have the word **dog.**

Who has the verb in
"He clipped his nails"?

I have the word **call.**

Who has the verb in
"Please pour the milk"?

I have the word **clipped.**

Who has the adjective in
"Her room is so messy"?

I have the word **pour.**

Who has the noun in
"He threw the ball"?

I have the word **messy.**

Who has the adjective in
"It's a stormy day"?

I have the word **ball.**

Who has the adjective in
"The tired baby napped"?

I have the word **stormy.**

Who has the verb in
"I see a green frog"?

Nouns, Verbs, and Adjectives

I have the word **see.**

Who has the adjective in "My account is empty"?

I have the word **book.**

Who has the adjective in "I saw a colorful quilt"?

I have the word **empty.**

Who has the verb in "I found the map"?

I have the word **colorful.**

Who has the verb in "Please eat all of your vegetables"?

I have the word **found.**

Who has the adjective in "The delicate vase broke"?

I have the word **eat.**

Who has the noun in "The train was running late"?

I have the word **delicate.**

Who has the verb in "Please recycle this"?

I have the word **train.**

Who has the adjective in "The ice cream made her hands feel sticky"?

I have the word **recycle.**

Who has the noun in "The book was checked out yesterday"?

I have the word **sticky.**

Who has the noun in "These socks are brand new"?

Nouns, Verbs, and Adjectives

I have the word **socks.**

Who has the noun in
"Let's go to the park"?

I have the word **bottle.**

Who has the adjective in
"That's a huge mountain"?

I have the word **park.**

Who has the verb in
"The plane departed on time"?

I have the word **huge.**

Who has the adjective in
"The sky is cloudy"?

I have the word **departed.**

Who has the adjective in
"The dress was expensive"?

I have the word **cloudy.**

Who has the noun in
"The rabbit quickly hopped away"?

I have the word **expensive.**

Who has the adjective in
"Unfortunately, the soup was cold"?

I have the word **rabbit.**

Who has the verb in
"Check your work"?

I have the word **cold.**

Who has the noun in
"Please recycle your bottle"?

I have the word **check.**

Who has the adjective in
"What an adorable baby"?

I Have, Who Has?: Language Arts • 5–6 © 2006 Creative Teaching Press

Nouns, Verbs, and Adjectives

I have the word **adorable.**

Who has the verb in
"The snow fell during the night"?

I have the word **rushed.**

Who has the adjective in
"The children are very noisy today"?

I have the word **fell.**

Who has the noun in
"I need my striped jacket"?

I have the word **noisy.**

Who has the verb in
"I play video games"?

I have the word **jacket.**

Who has the adjective in
"It was a sunny day"?

I have the word **play.**

Who has the noun in
"I'd like an ice cream please"?

I have the word **sunny.**

Who has the noun in
"I bought a new tennis racket"?

I have the word **ice cream.**

Who has the verb in
"Mya painted that picture"?

I have the word **racket.**

Who has the verb in
"She rushed to work this morning"?

I have the word **painted.**

Who has the first card?

I Have, Who Has?: Language Arts • 5–6 © 2006 Creative Teaching Press

Nouns, Verbs, and Adjectives

As your classmates identify each noun, verb, and adjective, lightly color in the matching box to uncover the hidden riddle and its answer. Listen closely so you don't miss any answers.

CLIPPED	PLAY	DELICATE	HUGE	DOG
COLD	PARK	WHY	SUNNY	STICKY
ARE	RECYCLE	BULLDOZER	BOTTLE	CHECK
MESSY	NOISY	SOCKS	TEDDY	FOUND
BEARS	TRAIN	TIRED	NEVER	RUSHED
CALL	EXPENSIVE	HUNGRY	EAT	RABBIT
BECAUSE	BOOK	RACKET	THEY	POUR
DEPARTED	ARE	CLOUDY	EMPTY	ICE CREAM
BALL	FELL	STORMY	ALWAYS	JACKET
STUFFED	COLORFUL	PAINTED	ADORABLE	SEE

Write the riddle and answer you uncovered.

_____

_____

Write three complete sentences. Use at least one of the nouns listed above in each sentence.

_____

_____

_____

Pronouns, Adjectives, and Adverbs

I have the **first card.**

Who has the adjective in "The inflated balloon popped"?

I have the word **broken.**

Who has the pronoun in "I will call Heather tonight"?

I have the word **inflated.**

Who has the adjective in "The filthy room was vacuumed by the maid"?

I have the word **I.**

Who has the adjective in "The organized files are in the drawer"?

I have the word **filthy.**

Who has the adverb in "The sheets were folded neatly by her father"?

I have the word **organized.**

Who has the pronoun in "Dan saw it run under the bed"?

I have the word **neatly.**

Who has the adverb in "They anxiously waited for the plane to arrive"?

I have the word **it.**

Who has the pronoun in "She dances gracefully"?

I have the word **anxiously.**

Who has the adjective in "Sam fixed the broken eyeglasses"?

I have the word **She.**

Who has the adverb in "She can easily solve the complicated problem"?

I Have, Who Has?: Language Arts • 5–6 © 2006 Creative Teaching Press

Pronouns, Adjectives, and Adverbs

I have the word **easily.**

Who has the adjective in "I prefer wheat bread with my eggs"?

I have the word **tired.**

Who has the adverb in "They promptly arrived at the office"?

I have the word **wheat.**

Who has the pronoun in "He found the lost hamster"?

I have the word **promptly.**

Who has the adjective in "The ferocious lion rested in the grass"?

I have the word **He.**

Who has the pronoun in "They went to the movies"?

I have the word **ferocious.**

Who has the adjective in "The sun was so bright today"?

I have the word **They.**

Who has the adverb in "They carefully opened the box"?

I have the word **bright.**

Who has the adjective in "The late train finally arrived"?

I have the word **carefully.**

Who has the adjective in "The tired mother rested"?

I have the word **late.**

Who has the adverb in "They proudly displayed their trophies"?

Pronouns, Adjectives, and Adverbs

I have the word **proudly**.

Who has the adverb in
"The tired lady rested quietly"?

I have the word **We**.

Who has the adjective in
"The recycled cans are in the bin"?

I have the word **quietly**.

Who has the pronoun in
"The bus drove right past them"?

I have the word **recycled**.

Who has the adverb in
"She slowly raised her hand"?

I have the word **them**.

Who has the adverb in
"He regretfully admitted
what he did wrong"?

I have the word **slowly**.

Who has the adverb in
"It bravely hunted for its prey"?

I have the word **regretfully**.

Who has the adverb in
"We'll be there shortly"?

I have the word **bravely**.

Who has the adverb in
"They happily played in the sand"?

I have the word **shortly**.

Who has the pronoun in
"We baked the cake"?

I have the word **happily**.

Who has the pronoun in
"You were late today"?

I Have, Who Has?: Language Arts • 5–6 © 2006 Creative Teaching Press

Pronouns, Adjectives, and Adverbs

I have the word **You.**

Who has the adjective in
"What a delicious brownie"?

I have the word **thoughtfully.**

Who has the pronoun in
"Jessica helped him wrap the gifts"?

I have the word **delicious.**

Who has the adverb in
"The crowd was cheering loudly"?

I have the word **him.**

Who has the adverb in
"They silently walked across
the dark hallway"?

I have the word **loudly.**

Who has the adverb in
"She rarely lost a game"?

I have the word **silently.**

Who has the adverb in
"The sports car rapidly drove
down the street"?

I have the word **rarely.**

Who has the adverb in
"The hungry squirrel quickly
collected nuts"?

I have the word **rapidly.**

Who has the adjective in
"This salsa is spicy"?

I have the word **quickly.**

Who has the adverb in
"She thoughtfully answered
the question"?

I have the word **spicy.**

Who has the first card?

I Have, Who Has?: Language Arts • 5–6 © 2006 Creative Teaching Press

Pronouns, Adjectives, and Adverbs

As your classmates identify each pronoun, adjective, and adverb, lightly color in the matching box to uncover the hidden riddle and its answer. Listen closely so you don't miss any answers.

RARELY	BRAVELY	INFLATED	THEY	REGRETFULLY
IT	RAPIDLY	FILTHY	HAPPILY	WHAT
DID	QUIETLY	NEATLY	RECYCLED	HE
CAREFULLY	THE	LOUDLY	THEM	SPIDER
SLOWLY	I	SHE	PROMPTLY	PROUDLY
DO	TIRED	ON	THOUGHTFULLY	THE
QUICKLY	WE	YOU	EASILY	SHORTLY
WHEAT	LATE	COMPUTER	HIM	MADE
ORGANIZED	A	FEROCIOUS	SILENTLY	BROKEN
SPICY	BRIGHT	WEBSITE	DELICIOUS	ANXIOUSLY

Write the riddle and answer you uncovered.

_____

Write three complete sentences. Use at least one of the words listed above in each sentence.

_____

_____

_____

I Have, Who Has?: Language Arts • 5–6 © 2006 Creative Teaching Press

Parts of Speech

I have the **first card.**

Who has the adverb in
"He rarely loses his keys"?

I have the word **rarely.**

Who has the noun in
"The cow began to moo"?

I have the word **cow.**

Who has the adjective in
"The frozen peas are on the counter"?

I have the word **frozen.**

Who has the preposition in
"The dog dug under the fence"?

I have the word **under.**

Who has the adjective in
"The rare snake is at the museum"?

I have the word **rare.**

Who has the plural noun in
"The hammers were hanging
on the wall"?

I have the word **hammers.**

Who has the preposition in
"I drove the tractor into the barn"?

I have the word **into.**

Who has the adverb in
"The snail slowly crawled
up the plant"?

I have the word **slowly.**

Who has the verb in
"He spoke politely to the teacher"?

I have the word **spoke.**

Who has the adjective in
"Her damp jacket was hanging
on the line"?

Parts of Speech

I have the word **damp.**

Who has the pronoun in
"He skied down the mountain"?

I have the word **poured.**

Who has the adjective in
"Its sharp nails scratched her"?

I have the word **He.**

Who has the adjective in
"The healthy baby is smiling"?

I have the word **sharp.**

Who has the pronoun in
"She loved the new necklace"?

I have the word **healthy.**

Who has the verb in
"He rushed to his meeting"?

I have the word **She.**

Who has the conjunction in
"We bought apples and oranges
at the market"?

I have the word **rushed.**

Who has the adverb in
"She quickly finished her work"?

I have the word **and.**

Who has the adjective in
"I threw the smelly socks
into the basket"?

I have the word **quickly.**

Who has the verb in
"She poured the hot chocolate
into her mug"?

I have the word **smelly.**

Who has the preposition in
"She loved the book about the
dancing dog"

I Have, Who Has?: Language Arts • 5–6 © 2006 Creative Teaching Press

Parts of Speech

I have the word **about.**

Who has the verb in
"He dusted the piano quickly"?

I have the word **cautiously.**

Who has the preposition in
"They ran around the block"?

I have the word **dusted.**

Who has the adjective in
"The vacant house was for sale"?

I have the word **around.**

Who has the adjective in
"The butterfly is symmetrical"?

I have the word **vacant.**

Who has the verb in
"They played cards all night long"?

I have the word **symmetrical.**

Who has the preposition in
"The plane flew over the mountain"?

I have the word **played.**

Who has the pronoun in
"We can sit by the window"?

I have the word **over.**

Who has the preposition in
"They live near the lake"?

I have the word **We.**

Who has the adverb in
"They cautiously looked in the closet"?

I have the word **near.**

Who has the noun in
"His feet are stinky"?

Parts of Speech

I have the word **feet.**

Who has the noun in
"The watch is broken"?

I have the word **before.**

Who has the preposition in
"The parade will be on Monday"?

I have the word **watch.**

Who has the adverb in
"She sang the song quietly to herself"?

I have the word **on.**

Who has the verb in
"The ducklings carefully followed
the mother duck"?

I have the word **quietly.**

Who has the preposition in
"We hiked through the forest"?

I have the word **followed.**

Who has the pronoun in
"They won the race"?

I have the word **through.**

Who has the adjective in
"The bald eagle soars through
the sky"?

I have the word **They.**

Who has the conjunction in
"Do you want a dog or a cat"?

I have the word **bald.**

Who has the preposition in
"She did her homework before
playing outside"?

I have the word **or.**

Who has the first card?

I Have, Who Has?: Language Arts • 5–6 © 2006 Creative Teaching Press

Parts of Speech

As your classmates identify each word, lightly color in the matching box to uncover the hidden riddle and its answer. Listen closely so you don't miss any answers.

HAMMERS	WHAT	INTO	QUIETLY	QUICKLY
DID	AROUND	POURED	THE	CAUTIOUSLY
RARE	SHARP	RARELY	GROUND	THROUGH
BALD	SAY	RUSHED	ABOUT	COW
SHE	WE	WATCH	SYMMETRICAL	FOLLOWED
OR	FROZEN	TO THE	SLOWLY	OVER
AND	THEY	DUSTED	EARTHQUAKE	HEALTHY
UNDER	PLAYED	YOU	HE	ON
CRACK	SPOKE	VACANT	BEFORE	DAMP
SMELLY	FEET	ME	NEAR	UP

Write the riddle and answer you uncovered.

_____

_____

Write three complete sentences. Use at least one word listed above in each sentence. Then underline the nouns, circle the verbs, and draw a box around any adjectives in the sentences you wrote.

_____

_____

_____

Prepositions and Conjunctions

I have the **first card.**

Who has the preposition in
"The boat was near the dock"?

I have the word **behind.**

Who has the conjunction in
"We can swim or build a sandcastle"?

I have the word **near.**

Who has the preposition in
"She's the leader of the band"?

I have the word **or.**

Who has the preposition in
"He loved the monkeys at the zoo"?

I have the word **of.**

Who has the preposition in
"He swam up the river"?

I have the word **at.**

Who has the conjunction in
"You'd better hurry if you
want to be on time"?

I have the word **up.**

Who has the preposition in
"The can is on the top shelf"?

I have the word **if.**

Who has the preposition in
"The submarine went under
the water"?

I have the word **on.**

Who has the preposition in
"He hid behind the tree"?

I have the word **under.**

Who has the preposition in
"He waited quietly outside the
classroom"?

I Have, Who Has?: Language Arts • 5–6 © 2006 Creative Teaching Press

Prepositions and Conjunctions

I have the word **outside**.

Who has the conjunction in "You can sit here as long as you wear a seatbelt"?

I have the word **down**.

Who has the conjunction in "Clean your room, otherwise you can't go"?

I have the words **as long as**.

Who has the conjunction in "He went to school and studied hard"?

I have the word **otherwise**.

Who has the conjunction in "Open the door, but please be quiet"?

I have the word **and**.

Who has the conjunction in "He was tired, yet he kept practicing"?

I have the word **but**.

Who has the preposition in "He fell off the ladder"?

I have the word **yet**.

Who has the preposition in "The butterflies flew above the nets"?

I have the word **off**.

Who has the preposition in "He drove over the bridge"?

I have the word **above**.

Who has the preposition in "Jill ran down the hill"?

I have the word **over**.

Who has the conjunction in "She wouldn't have any clothes, unless they found her luggage"?

Prepositions and Conjunctions

I have the word **unless.**

Who has the conjunction in "He gets further into debt whenever he goes shopping"?

I have the word **into.**

Who has the preposition in "He rested underneath the canopy"?

I have the word **whenever.**

Who has the preposition in "He had food caught between his teeth"?

I have the word **underneath.**

Who has the preposition in "The boy walked around the mud puddle"?

I have the word **between.**

Who has the preposition in "He got back from his vacation yesterday"?

I have the word **around.**

Who has the conjunction in "The coffee was cold, so she warmed it in the microwave"?

I have the word **from.**

Who has the preposition in "We ran toward the soccer field"?

I have the word **so.**

Who has the preposition in "The boxes are below the cans"?

I have the word **toward.**

Who has the preposition in "She put the cake into the warm oven"?

I have the word **below.**

Who has the preposition in "They slept inside the fancy hotel"?

I Have, Who Has?: Language Arts • 5–6 © 2006 Creative Teaching Press

Prepositions and Conjunctions

I have the word **inside.**

Who has the conjunction in "She bought the house although it was expensive"?

I have the word **beside.**

Who has the conjunction in "It rained all day; however, we still had fun"?

I have the word **although.**

Who has the conjunction in "We helped our friends because they were hurt"?

I have the word **however.**

Who has the conjunction in "You wait here while I go to buy a newspaper"?

I have the word **because.**

Who has the preposition in "The book was about dinosaurs"?

I have the word **while.**

Who has the preposition in "He ate cookies instead of tasting the pie"?

I have the word **about.**

Who has the conjunction in "We won't get dessert until we eat the carrots"?

I have the words **instead of.**

Who has the preposition in "We were quiet during the concert"?

I have the word **until.**

Who has the preposition in "He sat beside his sister"?

I have the word **during.**

Who has the first card?

I Have, Who Has?: Language Arts • 5–6 © 2006 Creative Teaching Press

Prepositions and Conjunctions

As your classmates identify each preposition and conjunction, lightly color in the matching box to uncover the hidden riddle and its answer. Listen closely so you don't miss any answers.

BETWEEN	WHY	FROM	DID	AND
THE	UNLESS	COOKIE	AS LONG AS	GO
WHENEVER	DURING	OVER	OUTSIDE	UNTIL
TOWARD	IF	BESIDE	ABOUT	TO
THE	OFF	UNDER	BECAUSE	ALTHOUGH
HOSPITAL	BEHIND	AT	BUT	IT
INTO	UNDERNEATH	OTHERWISE	HOWEVER	INSIDE
FELT	ON	OR	DOWN	CRUMBY
UP	WHILE	AROUND	ABOVE	INSTEAD OF
NEAR	OF	SO	BELOW	YET

Write the riddle and answer you uncovered.

_____

_____

Write three complete sentences. Use at least one of the prepositions or conjunctions listed above in each sentence. Then underline the prepositions and circle the conjunctions in the sentences you wrote.

_____

_____

_____

I Have, Who Has?: Language Arts • 5–6 © 2006 Creative Teaching Press

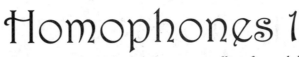

* Note: For this game students find the correct spelling for each homophone.

I have the **first card.**

Who has **blew** as in
"He blew the whistle"?

I have the homophone
spelled **c - a - r - e - t.**

Who has **aunts** as in
"Her aunts and uncles were
late for dinner"?

I have the homophone
spelled **b - l - e - w.**

Who has **two** as in
"She ate two cookies"?

I have the homophone
spelled **a - u - n - t - s.**

Who has **add** as in
"Don't forget to add the tax
to the total cost"?

I have the homophone
spelled **t - w - o.**

Who has **tale** as in
"We read the tale of The Boy
Who Cried Wolf"?

I have the homophone
spelled **a - d - d.**

Who has **dew** as in
"The morning dew glistened
on the grass"?

I have the homophone
spelled **t - a - l - e.**

Who has **eight** as in
"His favorite number is eight"?

I have the homophone
spelled **d - e - w.**

Who has **wood** as in
"This bench is made out of wood"?

I have the homophone
spelled **e - i - g - h - t.**

Who has **caret** as in
"Remember to use a caret
when you revise your writing"?

I have the homophone
spelled **w - o - o - d.**

Who has **chord** as in
"Please play the next chord
on the piano"?

Homophones 1

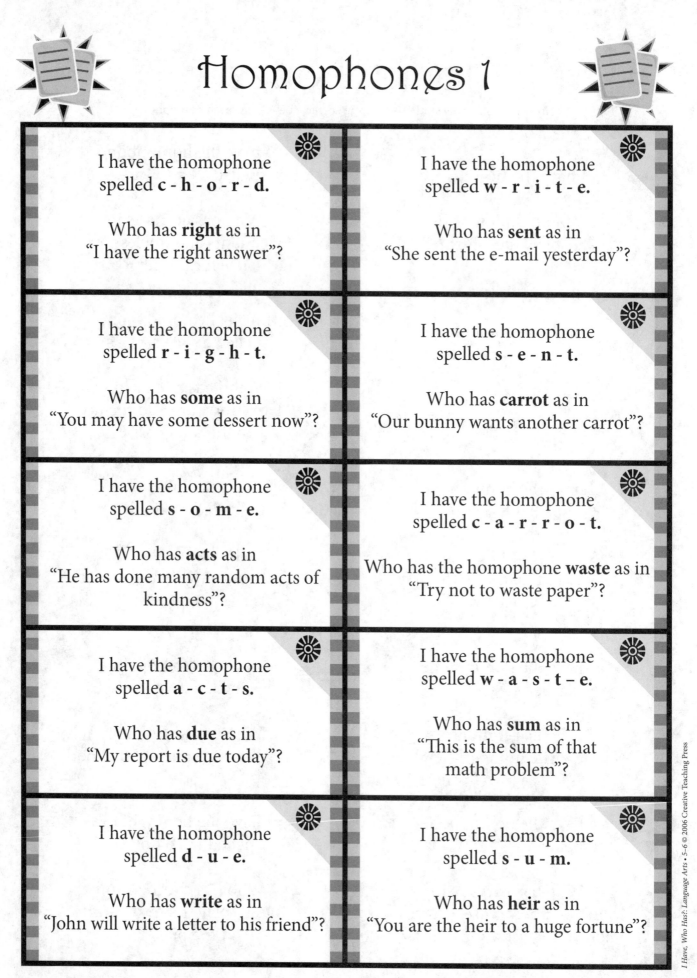

I have the homophone
spelled **c - h - o - r - d.**

Who has **right** as in
"I have the right answer"?

I have the homophone
spelled **w - r - i - t - e.**

Who has **sent** as in
"She sent the e-mail yesterday"?

I have the homophone
spelled **r - i - g - h - t.**

Who has **some** as in
"You may have some dessert now"?

I have the homophone
spelled **s - e - n - t.**

Who has **carrot** as in
"Our bunny wants another carrot"?

I have the homophone
spelled **s - o - m - e.**

Who has **acts** as in
"He has done many random acts of
kindness"?

I have the homophone
spelled **c - a - r - r - o - t.**

Who has the homophone **waste** as in
"Try not to waste paper"?

I have the homophone
spelled **a - c - t - s.**

Who has **due** as in
"My report is due today"?

I have the homophone
spelled **w - a - s - t – e.**

Who has **sum** as in
"This is the sum of that
math problem"?

I have the homophone
spelled **d - u - e.**

Who has **write** as in
"John will write a letter to his friend"?

I have the homophone
spelled **s - u - m.**

Who has **heir** as in
"You are the heir to a huge fortune"?

I Have, Who Has?: Language Arts • 5–6 © 2006 Creative Teaching Press

Homophones 1

I have the homophone
spelled **h - e - i - r.**

Who has **thrown** as in
"The trash was thrown away"?

I have the homophone
spelled **t - o.**

Who has **axe** as in
"The axe is in the shed with
the other tools"?

I have the homophone
spelled **t - h - r - o - w - n.**

Who has **would** as in
"I would like more cake"?

I have the homophone
spelled **a - x - e.**

Who has **cent** as in
"That's not worth one cent"?

I have the homophone
spelled **w - o - u - l - d.**

Who has **threw** as in
"She threw it away"?

I have the homophone
spelled **c - e - n - t.**

Who has **air** as in
"The balloon is full or air"?

I have the homophone
spelled **t - h - r - e - w.**

Who has **too** as in
"The belt was too big for her waist"?

I have the homophone
spelled **a - i - r.**

Who has **ate** as in
"I think that frog just ate a fly"?

I have the homophone
spelled **t - o - o.**

Who has **to** as in
"I went to the store"?

I have the homophone
spelled **a - t - e.**

Who has **blue** as in
"Here are your blue jeans"?

I Have, Who Has?: Language Arts • 5–6 © 2006 Creative Teaching Press

Homophones 1

I have the homophone
spelled **b - l - u - e**.

Who has **wear** as in
"I will wear my new shoes today"?

I have the homophone
spelled **t - h - r - o - n - e**.

Who has **ants** as in
"The ants were crawling
on the cookie"?

I have the homophone
spelled **w - e - a - r**.

Who has **ad** as in
"The ad on television is for a new
cereal"?

I have the homophone
spelled **a - n - t - s**.

Who has **through** as in
"They ran through the field"?

I have the homophone
spelled **a - d**.

Who has **cord** as in
"The cord was tied around the box"?

I have the homophone
spelled **t - h - r - o - u - g - h**.

Who has **hare** as in
"We read the fable called
The Tortoise and the Hare"?

I have the homophone
spelled **c - o - r - d**.

Who has **hair** as in
"She brushed her hair"?

I have the homophone
spelled **h - a - r - e**.

Who has **scent** as in
"The candle has a vanilla scent"?

I have the homophone
spelled **h - a - i - r**.

Who has **throne** as in
"The king sat on his throne"?

I have the homophone
spelled **s - c - e - n – t**.

Who has the first card?

I Have, Who Has?: Language Arts • 5–6 © 2006 Creative Teaching Press

Homophones 1

As your classmates identify each homophone, lightly color in the matching box to uncover the hidden riddle and its answer. Listen closely so you don't miss any answers.

WHO	BLEW	AD	WALKS	SUM
ADD	WASTE	DEW	WRITE	IN
THREW	THE	CENT	SCENT	CORD
DUE	CHORD	WEAR	TWO	WOOD
HEIR	WOODS	AIR	ANTS	ATE
BLUE	TALE	RIGHT	WITH	AUNTS
NOTHING	WOULD	TOO	AXE	CARROT
ACTS	ON	THROUGH	EIGHT	A
HARE	CARET	SENT	BARE	THRONE
THROWN	BEAR	HAIR	TO	SOME

Write the riddle and answer you uncovered.

_____

Write three complete sentences. Use a pair of homophones in each sentence. Circle the homophones.

_____

_____

_____

I Have, Who Has?: Language Arts • 5–6 © 2006 Creative Teaching Press

Homophones 2

*Note: For this game students find the correct spelling for each homophone.

I have the **first card.**

Who has **no** as in
"Noah answered no when he was
asked if he likes spiders"?

I have the homophone
spelled **p - e - a - c - e.**

Who has **urn** as in
"Please put the flowers in the urn"?

I have the homophone
spelled **n - o.**

Who has **steel** as in
"The bridge was built with steel"?

I have the homophone
spelled **u - r - n.**

Who has **led** as in
"The horse was led into the barn"?

I have the homophone
spelled **s - t - e - e - l.**

Who has **know** as in
"I know how to play the flute"?

I have the homophone
spelled **l - e - d.**

Who has **reign** as in
"The king will reign another ten years"?

I have the homophone
spelled **k – n - o - w.**

Who has **tax** as in
"The sales tax was raised a penny"?

I have the homophone
spelled **r - e - i - g - n.**

Who has **stair** as in
"She is sitting on the last stair"?

I have the homophone
spelled **t - a - x.**

Who has **peace** as in
"There was a time of peace
after the war"?

I have the homophone
spelled **s - t - a - i - r.**

Who has **pail** as in
"Please put some water in that pail"?

I Have, Who Has?: Language Arts • 5–6 © 2006 Creative Teaching Press

Homophones 2

I have the homophone
spelled **p - a - i - l**.

Who has **piece** as in
"He ate a large piece of cake"?

I have the homophone
spelled **m - a - i - l**.

Who has **kernel** as in
"Every kernel of popcorn
actually popped"?

I have the homophone
spelled **p - i - e - c - e**.

Who has **rain** as in
"The weather forecaster says
it's going to rain tomorrow"?

I have the homophone
spelled **k - e - r - n - e - l**.

Who has **pale** as in
"Her face looked so pale
when she saw the spider"?

I have the homophone
spelled **r - a - i - n**.

Who has **stare** as in
"It's rude to stare at people"?

I have the homophone
spelled **p - a - l - e**.

Who has **fair** as in
"I don't think that's a fair decision"?

I have the homophone
spelled **s - t - a - r - e**.

Who has **heal** as in
"This medicine will help
your wound heal"?

I have the homophone
spelled **f - a - i - r**.

Who has **male** as in
"The new puppy is a male,
not a female"?

I have the homophone
spelled **h - e - a - l**.

Who has **mail** as in
"The mail was delivered on time"?

I have the homophone
spelled **m - a - l - e**.

Who has **colonel** as in
"He was a colonel in the army"?

I Have, Who Has?: Language Arts • 5–6 © 2006 Creative Teaching Press

Homophones 2

I have the homophone
spelled **c - o -l - o - n - e - l.**

Who has **fir** as in
"That table is made from
wood from a fir tree"?

I have the homophone
spelled **s - t - e - a - l.**

Who has **fur** as in
"The dog's fur got wet in the rain"?

I have the homophone
spelled **f - i - r.**

Who has **pause** as in
"We will now pause for a
moment of silence"?

I have the homophone
spelled **f - u - r.**

Who has **heel** as in
"I have a blister on my heel"?

I have the homophone
spelled **p - a - u - s - e.**

Who has **earn** as in
"He will earn a lot of money
at his new job"?

I have the homophone
spelled **h - e - e - l.**

Who has **paws** as in
"The cat's paws were dirty"?

I have the homophone
spelled **e - a - r - n.**

Who has **pier** as in
"He walked along the pier"?

I have the homophone
spelled **p - a - w - s.**

Who has **haul** as in
"They had to haul the old mattress to
the dump"?

I have the homophone
spelled **p - i - e - r.**

Who has **steal** as in
"It's dishonest to steal"?

I have the homophone
spelled **h - a - u - l.**

Who has **made** as in
"Look what I made"?

I Have, Who Has?: Language Arts • 5–6 © 2006 Creative Teaching Press

Homophones 2

I have the homophone
spelled **m - a - d - e.**

Who has **fare** as in
"The train fare is so expensive"?

I have the homophone
spelled **l - e - a - s - e - d.**

Who has **tacks** as in
"She got new tacks for her
bulletin board"?

I have the homophone
spelled **f - a - r - e.**

Who has **maid** as in
"I wish we had a butler or a maid"?

I have the homophone
spelled **t - a - c - k - s.**

Who has **peer** as in
"He's your peer since you are
the same age"?

I have the homophone
spelled **m - a - i - d.**

Who has **hall** as in
"The guest room is right
down the hall"?

I have the homophone
spelled **p - e - e - r.**

Who has **nose** as in
"Her nose was bleeding"?

I have the homophone
spelled **h - a - l - l.**

Who has **lead** as in
"I broke the lead of my pencil"?

I have the homophone
spelled **n - o - s - e.**

Who has **least** as in
"The youngest sister got the least
amount of dessert"?

I have the homophone
spelled **l - e - a - d.**

Who has **leased** as in
"They leased a new apartment"?

I have the homophone
spelled **l - e - a - s - t.**

Who has the first card?

I Have, Who Has?: Language Arts • 5–6 © 2006 Creative Teaching Press

Homophones 2

As your classmates identify each homophone, lightly color in the matching box to uncover the hidden riddle and its answer. Listen closely so you don't miss any answers.

HALL	NO	WHAT'S	MAID	HEAL
RAIN	EARN	FARE	REIGN	AN
EQUINE	CREATURE	STEAL	PIER	LEAD
STARE	PIECE	STEEL	LEAST	LED
LOSING	PALE	PAUSE	LEASED	ITS
KNOW	FUR	MADE	URN	PEER
VOICE	HEEL	CALLED	HAUL	MAIL
NOSE	PEACE	KERNEL	TACKS	A
TAX	HOARSE	PAIL	FAIR	STAIR
FIR	PAWS	COLONEL	HORSE	MALE

Write the riddle and answer you uncovered.

_____

Write two homophone riddles of your own. Circle the homophones.

_____

_____

I Have, Who Has?: Language Arts • 5–6 © 2006 Creative Teaching Press

Similes 1

I have the **first card.**

Who has the best word for the simile "I can't hear him. He's as quiet as a _____"?

I have the word **fox.**

Who has the best word for the simile "What a beautiful ring! It's shines like the _____"?

I have the word **mouse.**

Who has the best word for the simile "She's as stubborn as a _____"?

I have the word **sun.**

Who has the best word for the simile "I cleaned my room! It's as clean as a _____"?

I have the word **mule.**

Who has the best word for the simile "Does anything wake him up? He sleeps like a _____"?

I have the word **whistle.**

Who has the best word for the simile "I'm so thirsty. My mouth feels as dry as a _____"?

I have the word **baby.**

Who has the best word for the simile "When he sleeps he roars like a _____"?

I have the word **bone.**

Who has the best word for the simile "I can do that division problem. It's as easy as _____"?

I have the word **lion.**

Who has the best word for the simile "What a sneaky thing to do! She is as sly as a _____"?

I have the word **pie.**

Who has the best word for the simile "He would never lie. He's as straight as an _____"?

I Have, Who Has?: Language Arts • 5–6 © 2006 Creative Teaching Press

Similes 1

I have the word **arrow**.

Who has the best word for the simile "He's as snug as a _____"?

I have the word **weed**.

Who has the best word for the simile "He's so smart! He's as sharp as a _____"?

I have the words **bug in a rug**.

Who has the best word for the simile "The starched shirt is as stiff as a _____"?

I have the word **tack**.

Who has the best word for the simile "My stomach is so full that it's as hard as a _____"?

I have the word **board**.

Who has the best word for the simile "She was so scared that she was as pale as a _____"?

I have the word **rock**.

Who has the best word for the simile "That puppy is just as cute as a _____"?

I have the word **ghost**.

Who has the best word for the simile "Your eyes are as blue as the _____"?

I have the word **button**.

Who has the best word for the simile "The stout man was as round as a _____"?

I have the word **sky**.

Who has the best word for the simile "I can't believe you outgrew those pants already. You seem to grow like a _____"?

I have the word **barrel**.

Who has the best word for the simile "The winter cabin was as cold as _____"?

I Have, Who Has?: Language Arts • 5–6 © 2006 Creative Teaching Press

Similes 1

I have the word **ice.**

Who has the best word for the simile "The girl is as happy as a _____"?

I have the word **lamb.**

Who has the best word for the simile "The acrobat seems to swing like a _____"?

I have the word **lark.**

Who has the best word for the simile "That tire is as flat as a _____"?

I have the word **monkey.**

Who has the best word for the simile "He's never hungry. In fact, he eats like a _____"?

I have the word **pancake.**

Who has the best word for the simile "He seems to leap like a _____"?

I have the word **bird.**

Who has the best word for the simile "Those dirty shoes are as smelly as a _____"?

I have the word **frog.**

Who has the best word for the simile "The ballerina was as graceful as a _____"?

I have the word **skunk.**

Who has the best word for the simile "He was so scared that he was shaking like a _____"?

I have the word **swan.**

Who has the best word for the simile "She's as gentle as a _____"?

I have the word **leaf.**

Who has the best word for the simile "Her personality is as sweet as _____"?

Similes 1

I have the word **sugar.**

Who has the best word for the simile "He's always last. In fact, he's as slow as a _____"?

I have the word **eel.**

Who has the best word for the simile "She's as busy as a _____"?

I have the word **turtle.**

Who has the best word for the simile "Wow! He carried that? He's as strong as an _____"?

I have the word **bee.**

Who has the best word for the simile "He ran so quickly in the race! He was as fast as a _____"?

I have the word **ox.**

Who has the best word for the simile "The man on the deserted island was as hungry as a _____"?

I have the word **jet.**

Who has the best word for the simile "The painting was as colorful as a _____"?

I have the word **bear.**

Who has the best word for the simile "Her hair felt as smooth as _____"?

I have the word **rainbow.**

Who has the best word for the simile "You're not heavy at all. I think you're as light as a _____"?

I have the word **silk.**

Who has the best word for the simile "The goo was as slimy as an _____"?

I have the word **feather.**

Who has the first card?

I Have, Who Has?: Language Arts • 5–6 © 2006 Creative Teaching Press

Similes 1

As your classmates identify the word that completes each simile, lightly color in the matching box to uncover the hidden riddle and its answer. Listen closely so you don't miss any answers.

GHOST	WHERE	PIE	SKUNK	SHOULD
LARK	EEL	ICE	BEE	MULE
SUGAR	MOUSE	SKY	BIRD	YOU
WHISTLE	NEVER	WEED	TURTLE	TACK
TAKE	BUG IN A RUG	A	BONE	JET
PANCAKE	DOG	MONKEY	TO	ARROW
SUN	SILK	BABY	OX	LAMB
A	BOARD	BARREL	SWAN	FEATHER
BEAR	FROG	FLEA	LION	MARKET
FOX	ROCK	LEAF	RAINBOW	BUTTON

Write the riddle and answer you uncovered.

_____

_____

Write three sentences that include similes. Underline the simile in each sentence.

_____

_____

_____

Similes 2

I have the **first card.**

Who has the best word for the simile "The sandwich was huge. It was as big as a ____"?

I have the word **fiddle**.

Who has the best word for the simile "She could rock climb, surf, and ski cross-country by the age of nine. She was as tough as ____"?

I have the word **bus.**

Who has the best word for the simile "His directions confused me. They were as clear as ____"?

I have the word **nails.**

Who has the best word for the simile " He wouldn't admit that he lied even after having his mouth washed out with soap. He was as stubborn as a ____"?

I have the word **mud.**

Who has the best word for the simile "The contestant on the game show was so smart! He was as wise as an ____"?

I have the word **mule.**

Who has the best word for the simile "The fly was as dead as a ____"?

I have the word **owl.**

Who has the best word for the simile "Walking into the dark room, she felt like she was as blind as a ____"?

I have the word **doornail.**

Who has the best word for the simile "He was so tricky! He was like a wolf in ____"?

I have the word **bat.**

Who has the best word for the simile "He exercises every day. He is as fit as a ____"?

I have the words **sheep's clothing.**

Who has the best word for the simile "Her fever just wouldn't go down. She was as sick as a ____"?

I Have, Who Has?: Language Arts • 5–6 © 2006 Creative Teaching Press

Similes 2

I have the word **dog**.

Who has the best word for the simile "The jaguar was as black as ___"?

I have the word **peacock**.

Who has the best word for the simile "He sharpened the pencil so much that the tip of the lead was as sharp as a ___"?

I have the word **night**.

Who has the best word for the simile "It took her forever to get ready in the morning. She was as slow as ___"?

I have the word **needle**.

Who has the best word for the simile "Her shirt was red, green, blue, and yellow. It was as colorful as a ___"?

I have the word **molasses**.

Who has the best word for the simile "He was so incredibly thin that his mother said he was as skinny as a ___"?

I have the words **box of crayons**.

Who has the best word for the simile "She was always as busy as a ___"?

I have the word **rail**.

Who has the best word for the simile "The ice skater was as graceful as a ___"?

I have the word **beaver**.

Who has the best word for the simile "She admitted that her room was as messy as a ___"?

I have the word **swan**.

Who has the best word for the simile "After winning the gold medal, he was as proud as a ___"?

I have the word **pigsty**.

Who has the best word for the simile "The parchment letter was as fragile as a ___"?

Similes 2

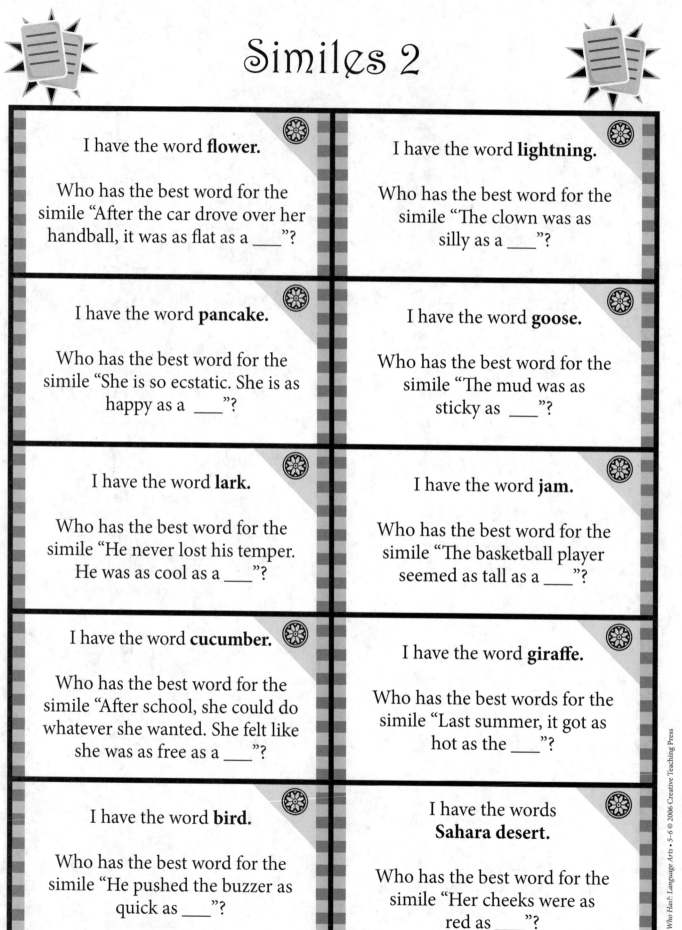

I have the word **flower**.

Who has the best word for the simile "After the car drove over her handball, it was as flat as a ___"?

I have the word **lightning**.

Who has the best word for the simile "The clown was as silly as a ___"?

I have the word **pancake**.

Who has the best word for the simile "She is so ecstatic. She is as happy as a ___"?

I have the word **goose**.

Who has the best word for the simile "The mud was as sticky as ___"?

I have the word **lark**.

Who has the best word for the simile "He never lost his temper. He was as cool as a ___"?

I have the word **jam**.

Who has the best word for the simile "The basketball player seemed as tall as a ___"?

I have the word **cucumber**.

Who has the best word for the simile "After school, she could do whatever she wanted. She felt like she was as free as a ___"?

I have the word **giraffe**.

Who has the best words for the simile "Last summer, it got as hot as the ___"?

I have the word **bird**.

Who has the best word for the simile "He pushed the buzzer as quick as ___"?

I have the words **Sahara desert**.

Who has the best word for the simile "Her cheeks were as red as ___"?

I Have, Who Has?: Language Arts • 5–6 © 2006 Creative Teaching Press

Similes 2

I have the word **roses.**

Who has the best word for the simile "The main character was so crazy! He was as mad as a ___"?

I have the word **fur.**

Who has the best word for the simile "The new shoes were as green as ___"?

I have the word **hatter.**

Who has the best word for the simile "She was as playful as a ___"?

I have the word **grass.**

Who has the best word for the simile "The girl is as rich as a ___"?

I have the word **kitten.**

Who has the best words for the simile "They lived paycheck to paycheck. He felt like he was as poor as a ___"?

I have the word **queen.**

Who has the best words for the simile "The classroom was as noisy as a ___"?

I have the words **church mouse.**

Who has the best word for the simile "He said he'd be back as quick as a ___"?

I have the words **herd of elephants.**

Who has the best word for the simile "Her vision is so good that she seems to have eyes like a ___"?

I have the word **flash.**

Who has the best word for the simile "Her new sweater was as soft as a puppy's ___"?

I have the word **hawk.**

Who has the first card?

Similes 2

As your classmates identify the word that completes each simile, lightly color in the matching box to uncover the hidden riddle and its answer. Listen closely so you don't miss any answers.

SWAN	FUR	MUD	HATTER	PEACOCK
HOW ARE	PANCAKE	TIGERS	NIGHT	LIKE
OWL	DOG	ROSES	SERGEANTS	LARK
DOORNAIL	IN	RAIL	GIRAFFE	BUS
THE	JAM	ARMY	FLOWER	HAWK
MULE	FLASH	SHEEP'S CLOTHING	GRASS	KITTEN
BAT	PIGSTY	THEY	BOTH	MOLASSES
GOOSE	HAVE	LIGHTNING	NAILS	QUEEN
STRIPES	FIDDLE	BIRD	HERD OF ELEPHANTS	CUCUMBER
BOX OF CRAYONS	CHURCH MOUSE	NEEDLE	SAHARA DESERT	BEAVER

Write the riddle and answer you uncovered.

_____

Write three sentences that include similes. Underline the simile in each sentence.

_____

_____

_____

I Have, Who Has?: Language Arts • 5–6 © 2006 Creative Teaching Press

Idioms

I have the **first card.**

Who has the meaning of the idiom "I get the picture"?

I have **"He is depressed today."**

Who has the meaning of the idiom "He was between a rock and a hard place"?

I have **"I understand."**

Who has the meaning of the idiom "He talks a mile a minute"?

I have **"He had a very difficult decision to make."**

Who has the meaning of the idiom "He finished in the eleventh hour"?

I have **"He talks so fast!"**

Who has the meaning of the idiom "She's so wishy washy"?

I have **"He finished at the last possible moment."**

Who has the meaning of the idiom "She's a couch potato"?

I have **"She is constantly changing her mind."**

Who has the meaning of the idiom "You bit off more than you could chew"?

I have **"She sits around all day doing nothing."**

Who has the meaning of the idiom "I'm all ears"?

I have **"You took on more tasks than you could handle."**

Who has the meaning of the idiom "He is down in the dumps today"?

I have **"I'm ready to listen carefully."**

Who has the meaning of the idiom "He wants to foot the bill"?

I Have, Who Has?: Language Arts • 5–6 © 2006 Creative Teaching Press

Idioms

I have **"He wants to pay."**

Who has the meaning of the idiom "It will knock your socks off"?

I have **"Let's go eat."**

Who has the meaning of the idiom "She's the head honcho"?

I have **"You'll be amazed!"**

Who has the meaning of the idiom "It's time to hit the books"?

I have **"She's the boss."**

Who has the meaning of the idiom "I'm going to ace that test"?

I have **"It's time to study."**

Who has the meaning of the idiom "She was feeling under the weather"?

I have **"I am going to get an A."**

Who has the meaning of the idiom "His checking account was in the red"?

I have **"She was sick."**

Who has the meaning of the idiom "I'll give you my two cents worth"?

I have **"He owed more money than he had."**

Who has the meaning of the idiom "Try not to jump the gun"?

I have **"I'll tell you my opinion."**

Who has the meaning of the idiom "Let's go grab a bite"?

I have **"Try not to rush into something too quickly."**

Who has the meaning of the idiom "You need to cut it out right now"?

I Have, Who Has?: Language Arts • 5–6 © 2006 Creative Teaching Press

Idioms

I have **"You need to stop."**

Who has the meaning of the idiom "Get off my back"?

I have **"She thought it was funny."**

Who has the meaning of the idiom "She's driving me up the wall"?

I have **"Leave me alone."**

Who has the meaning of the idiom "I need you to pitch in"?

I have **"She's bothering me."**

Who has the meaning of the idiom "He did a bang-up job"?

I have **"I need you to help."**

Who has the meaning of the idiom "That jacket costs an arm and a leg"?

I have **"He did very well."**

Who has the meaning of the idiom "He was in the doghouse"?

I have **"It's very expensive."**

Who has the meaning of the idiom "It's time to hit the sack"?

I have **"He got in trouble and was being punished."**

Who has the meaning of the idiom "It's a piece of cake"?

I have **"It's bedtime."**

Who has the meaning of the idiom "She got a kick out of that"?

I have **"It's so easy."**

Who has the meaning of the idiom "You need to zip your lip"?

Idioms

I have **"You need to be quiet."**

Who has the meaning of the idiom "You're up a creek without a paddle"?

I have **"Help me."**

Who has the meaning of the idiom "I'm bushed"?

I have **"You have a problem and don't have an easy solution."**

Who has the meaning of the idiom "You need to hold your horses"?

I have **"I'm tired."**

Who has the meaning of the idiom "Keep your fingers crossed"?

I have **"You need to be patient."**

Who has the meaning of the idiom "I would stick my neck out for you"?

I have **"Keep hoping."**

Who has the meaning of the idiom "My eyes were bigger than my stomach"?

I have **"I would take a risk to help you."**

Who has the meaning of the idiom "Step on it"?

I have **"I ate too much."**

Who has the meaning of the idiom "She eats like a bird"?

I have **"Hurry."**

Who has the meaning of the idiom "Lend me a hand"?

I have **"She doesn't eat much."**

Who has the first card?

I Have, Who Has?: Language Arts • 5–6 © 2006 Creative Teaching Press

Idioms

As your classmates identify the meaning of each idiom, lightly color in the matching box to uncover the hidden riddle and its answer. Listen closely so you don't miss any answers.

I'M TIRED.	IT'S SO EASY.	I UNDERSTAND.	HE DID VERY WELL.	HELP ME.
YOU NEED TO BE QUIET.	WHEN	YOU NEED TO BE PATIENT.	HE TALKS SO FAST!	IS
HE HAD A VERY DIFFICULT DECISION TO MAKE.	I'LL TELL YOU MY OPINION.	IT'S TIME TO STUDY.	THE	SHE'S BOTHERING ME.
I WOULD TAKE A RISK TO HELP YOU.	VETERINARIAN	TRY NOT TO RUSH INTO SOMETHING TOO QUICKLY.	SHE SITS AROUND ALL DAY DOING NOTHING.	HE GOT IN TROUBLE AND WAS BEING PUNISHED.
SHE'S THE BOSS.	SHE IS CONSTANTLY CHANGING HER MIND.	LET'S GO EAT.	HE WANTS TO PAY.	YOU'LL BE AMAZED!
I'M READY TO LISTEN CAREFULLY.	THE BUSIEST	HE FINISHED AT THE LAST POSSIBLE MOMENT.	YOU HAVE A PROBLEM AND DON'T HAVE AN EASY SOLUTION.	WHEN
HURRY.	HE OWED MORE MONEY THAN HE HAD.	IT'S BEDTIME.	YOU TOOK ON MORE TASKS THAN YOU COULD HANDLE.	SHE WAS SICK.
SHE THOUGHT IT WAS FUNNY.	HE IS DEPRESSED TODAY.	IT'S	RAINING	CATS
LEAVE ME ALONE.	IT'S VERY EXPENSIVE.	I AM GOING TO GET AN A.	I NEED YOU TO HELP.	YOU NEED TO STOP.
I ATE TOO MUCH.	AND	KEEP HOPING.	DOGS	SHE DOESN'T EAT MUCH.

Write the riddle and answer you uncovered.

_____

Name one person you would stick your neck out for and explain why.

_____

Describe in complete sentences a time your eyes were bigger than your stomach.

_____

I Have, Who Has? Language Arts • 5–6 © 2006 Creative Teaching Press

Meaning to Root/Prefix/Suffix

I have the **first card.**

Who has the root that means
"to speak"?

I have the root
neo.

Who has the root that means
"heat or temperature"?

I have the root
dict.

Who has the root that means
"to throw"?

I have the root
therm.

Who has the roots that mean
"write or writing"?

I have the root
ject.

Who has the root that means
"to carry"?

I have the roots
graph, scrib, and script.

Who has the suffix that means
"the study of"?

I have the root
port.

Who has the prefixes that mean
"one"?

I have the suffix
-ology.

Who has the roots that mean
"to measure"?

I have the prefixes
mono- and uni-.

Who has the root that means
"new"?

I have the roots
meter and metry.

Who has the suffix that means
"fear of"?

I Have, Who Has?: Language Arts • 5–6 © 2006 Creative Teaching Press

Meaning to Root/Prefix/Suffix

I have the suffix
-phobia.

Who has the prefix that means
"under, below, or less"?

I have the root
vis.

Who has the prefix that means
"four"?

I have the prefix
hypo-.

Who has the prefix that means
"over, beyond, or high"?

I have the prefix
quad-.

Who has the prefixes that mean
"around"?

I have the prefix
hyper-.

Who has the roots that mean
"to bend"?

I have the prefixes
circ- and circum-.

Who has the prefix that means
"three"?

I have the roots
flect and flex.

Who has the root that means
"to believe"?

I have the prefix
tri-.

Who has the prefix that means
"across or through"?

I have the root
cred.

Who has the root that means
"to see"?

I have the prefix
trans-.

Who has the prefix that means
"self"?

Meaning to Root/Prefix/Suffix

I have the prefix
auto-.

Who has the roots that mean
"earth or land"?

I have the prefix
post-.

Who has the prefix that means
"again"?

I have the roots
terr, terra, and geo.

Who has the prefix that means
"small"?

I have the prefix
re-.

Who has the prefix that means
"before"?

I have the prefix
micro-.

Who has the root that means
"form or shape"?

I have the prefix
pre-.

Who has the roots that mean
"life"?

I have the root
morph.

Who has the roots that mean
"sound or voice"?

I have the roots
bio, vit, and viv.

Who has the root that means
"pull"?

I have the roots
phon, phono, and phone.

Who has the prefix that means
"after"?

I have the root
tract.

Who has the roots that mean
"send"?

I Have, Who Has?: Language Arts • 5–6 © 2006 Creative Teaching Press

Meaning to Root/Prefix/Suffix

I have the roots
mis and mit.

Who has the root that means
"cut or separate"?

I have the roots
nav, naus, and naut.

Who has the roots that mean
"to turn"?

I have the root
sect.

Who has the roots that mean
"good or well"?

I have the roots
vers and vert.

Who has the root that means
"break"?

I have the roots
bene, ben, and bon.

Who has the root that means
"to build"?

I have the root
rupt.

Who has the roots that mean
"go or yield"?

I have the root
struct.

Who has the root that means
"friend or companion"?

I have the roots
cede, ceed, and cess.

Who has the roots that mean
"law or justice"?

I have the root
socio.

Who has the roots that mean
"relating to the sea, ships,
or travelers"?

I have the roots
jur, jus, and jud.

Who has the first card?

Meaning to Root/Prefix/Suffix

As your classmates identify each root, prefix, and suffix, lightly color in the matching box to uncover the hidden Greek proverb. Listen closely so you don't miss any answers.

BENE, BEN, AND BON	DICT	RE-	AUTO-	MIS AND MIT
HE WHO	VIS	STRUCT	HYPO-	CRED
GRAPH, SCRIB, AND SCRIPT	IS NOT	METER AND METRY	TRACT	RUPT
SATISFIED	TERR, TERRA, AND GEO	WITH A	POST-	-OLOGY
PHON, PHONO, AND PHONE	THERM	TRANS-	JECT	VERS AND VERT
JUR, JUS, AND JUD	-PHOBIA	CEDE, CEED, AND CESS	LITTLE	TRI-
QUAD-	WILL	MICRO-	FLECT AND FLEX	BIO, VIT, AND VIV
NOT	PORT	CIRC- AND CIRCUM-	BE	SATISFIED
MORPH	SECT	HYPER-	WITH	MONO- AND UNI-
NAV, NAUS, AND NAUT	NEO	SOCIO	PRE-	A LOT

Write the Greek proverb you uncovered.

_____

_____

Explain the famous Greek proverb you uncovered. Answer in complete sentences.

_____

_____

I Have, Who Has?: Language Arts • 5–6 © 2006 Creative Teaching Press

Root/Prefix/Suffix to Meaning

I have the **first card.**

Who has the meaning of the root
ped?

I have the meaning
"before."

Who has the meaning of the prefix
post-?

I have the meaning
"foot."

Who has the meaning of the roots
mani and manu?

I have the meaning
"after."

Who has the meaning of the suffix
-phobia?

I have the meaning
"hand."

Who has the meaning of the root
spec?

I have the meaning
"a fear of."

Who has the meaning of the suffix
-ology?

I have the meaning
"to see or look."

Who has the meaning of the root
dict?

I have the meaning
"the study of."

Who has the meaning of the root
ject?

I have the meaning
"to speak."

Who has the meaning of the prefix
pre-?

I have the meaning
"to throw."

Who has the meaning of the root
sect?

Root/Prefix/Suffix to Meaning

I have the meaning
"to cut or separate."

Who has the meaning of the roots
graph, scrib, and script?

I have the meaning
"life or live."

Who has the meaning of the prefix
re-?

I have the meaning
"write or writing."

Who has the meaning of the prefixes
mono- and uni-?

I have the meaning
"again."

Who has the meaning of the prefix
sub-?

I have the meaning
"one."

Who has the meaning of the prefixes
anti-, counter-, and contra-?

I have the meaning
"under or below."

Who has the meaning of the roots
jur, jus, and jud?

I have the meaning
"against or opposite."

Who has the meaning of the root
cred?

I have the meaning
"law or justice."

Who has the meaning of the roots
ben, bon, and bene?

I have the meaning
"to believe."

Who has the meaning of the roots
bio, viv, and vit?

I have the meaning
"good or well."

Who has the meaning of the roots
mal and male?

I Have, Who Has?: Language Arts • 5–6 © 2006 Creative Teaching Press

Root/Prefix/Suffix to Meaning

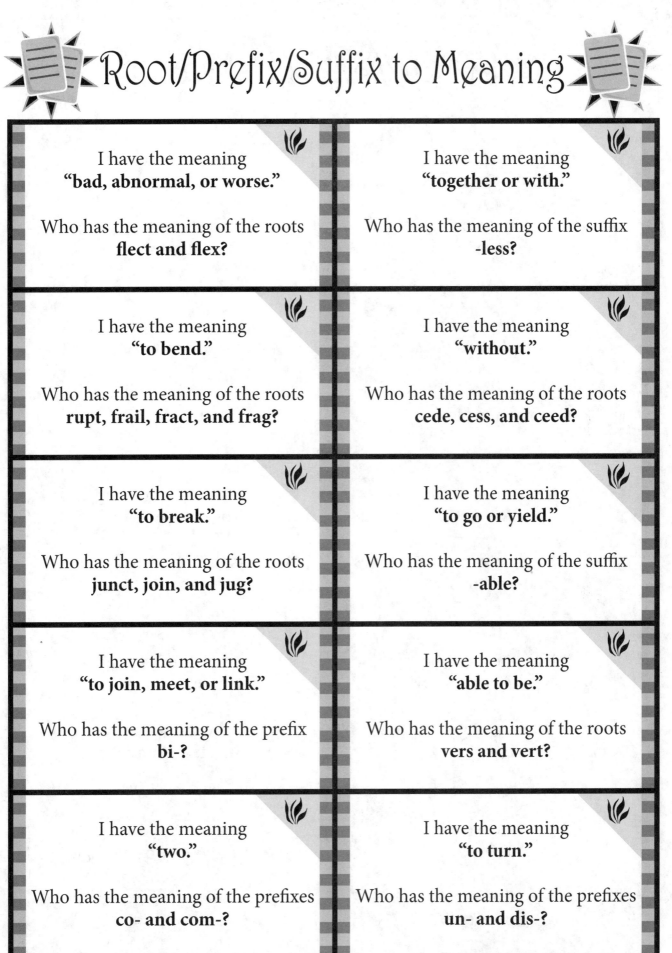

I have the meaning
"bad, abnormal, or worse."

Who has the meaning of the roots
flect and flex?

I have the meaning
"together or with."

Who has the meaning of the suffix
-less?

I have the meaning
"to bend."

Who has the meaning of the roots
rupt, frail, fract, and frag?

I have the meaning
"without."

Who has the meaning of the roots
cede, cess, and ceed?

I have the meaning
"to break."

Who has the meaning of the roots
junct, join, and jug?

I have the meaning
"to go or yield."

Who has the meaning of the suffix
-able?

I have the meaning
"to join, meet, or link."

Who has the meaning of the prefix
bi-?

I have the meaning
"able to be."

Who has the meaning of the roots
vers and vert?

I have the meaning
"two."

Who has the meaning of the prefixes
co- and com-?

I have the meaning
"to turn."

Who has the meaning of the prefixes
un- and dis-?

I Have, Who Has? Language Arts • 5–6 © 2006 Creative Teaching Press

Root/Prefix/Suffix to Meaning

I have the meaning
"not or none."

Who has the meaning of the root
struct?

I have the meaning
"within."

Who has the meaning of the root
therm?

I have the meaning
"to build."

Who has the meaning of the roots
terr, terra, and geo?

I have the meaning
"heat or temperature."

Who has the meaning of the prefixes
sym- and syn-?

I have the meaning
"land or earth."

Who has the meaning of the prefixes
mal- and mis-?

I have the meaning
"together or with."

Who has the meaning of the root
socio?

I have the meaning
"bad or badly, wrong, or ill."

Who has the meaning of the prefix
trans-?

I have the meaning
"friend or companion."

Who has the meaning of the roots
strain, string, and strict?

I have the meaning
"across."

Who has the meaning of the prefix
intra-?

I have the meaning
"to bind, tie, or draw tight."

Who has the first card?

I Have, Who Has?: Language Arts • 5–6 © 2006 Creative Teaching Press

Root/Prefix/Suffix to Meaning

As your classmates identify the meaning of each root, prefix, and suffix, lightly color in the matching box to uncover the hidden Latin phrase and its English translation. Listen closely so you don't miss any answers.

TO JOIN, MEET, OR LINK	FOOT	GOOD OR WELL	NOVUS	LAW OR JUSTICE
WRITE OR WRITING	ORDO	TO BIND, TIE, OR DRAW TIGHT	TO SEE OR LOOK	SECLORUM
WHICH	THE STUDY OF	MEANS	TO BEND	TWO
TO BREAK	WITHOUT	AGAINST OR OPPOSITE	LAND OR EARTH	TO THROW
TO SPEAK	HEAT OR TEMPERATURE	BAD, ABNORMAL, OR WORSE	TOGETHER OR WITH	BAD OR BADLY, WRONG, OR ILL
WITHIN	ONE	TOGETHER OR WITH	HAND	UNDER OR BELOW
A	ABLE TO BE	ACROSS	FRIEND OR COMPANION	TO TURN
BEFORE	NEW	A FEAR OF	TO GO OR YIELD	TO CUT OR SEPARATE
ORDER	TO BELIEVE	FOR	TO BUILD	NOT OR NONE
LIFE OR LIVE	THE	AFTER	AGES	AGAIN

Write the Latin phrase and English translation you uncovered.

_____

Explain in complete sentences what you think the Latin phrase means and why it's on the back of the United States dollar bill.

_____

Proverbs

I have the **first card.**

Who has the rest of the proverb "An apple a day . . ."?

I have **flock together.**

Who has the rest of the proverb "You can't have your cake and . . ."?

I have **keeps the doctor away.**

Who has the rest of the proverb "The grass is always greener . . ."?

I have **eat it too.**

Who has the rest of the proverb "Life is just a . . ."?

I have **on the other side of the fence.**

Who has the rest of the proverb "Beauty is only . . ."?

I have **bowl of cherries.**

Who has the rest of the proverb "All that glitters . . ."?

I have **skin deep.**

Who has the rest of the proverb "Don't count your chickens . . ."?

I have **is not gold.**

Who has the rest of the proverb "Look before you . . ."?

I have **before they hatch.**

Who has the rest of the proverb "Birds of a feather . . ."?

I have **leap.**

Who has the rest of the proverb "Great minds . . ."?

I Have, Who Has?: Language Arts • 5–6 © 2006 Creative Teaching Press

Proverbs

I have **think alike.**

Who has the rest of the proverb "A friend in need is a . . ."?

I have **May flowers.**

Who has the rest of the proverb "Bad news travels . . ."?

I have **friend indeed.**

Who has the rest of the proverb "Laughter is the best . . ."?

I have **fast.**

Who has the rest of the proverb "Better safe than . . ."?

I have **medicine.**

Who has the rest of the proverb "Ignorance . . ."?

I have **sorry.**

Who has the rest of the proverb "Ask no questions and . . ."?

I have **is bliss.**

Who has the rest of the proverb "Blood is thicker than . . ."?

I have **hear no lies.**

Who has the rest of the proverb "Love makes the world . . ."?

I have **water.**

Who has the rest of the proverb " April showers bring . . ."?

I have **go round.**

Who has the rest of the proverb "Money is the root of . . ."?

I Have, Who Has?: Language Arts • 5–6 © 2006 Creative Teaching Press

Proverbs

I have
all evils.

Who has the rest of the proverb
"When the cat is away . . ."?

I have
than words.

Who has the rest of the proverb
"Where there is a will . . ."?

I have
the mice will play.

Who has the rest of the proverb
"Two wrongs don't . . ."?

I have
there is a way.

Who has the rest of the proverb
"Don't look a gift horse . . ."?

I have
make a right.

Who has the rest of the proverb
"He who hesitates is . . ."?

I have
in the mouth.

Who has the rest of the proverb
"Seeing is . . ."?

I have
lost.

Who has the rest of the proverb
"You win some . . ."?

I have
believing.

Who has the rest of the proverb
"Finders keepers . . ."?

I have
you lose some.

Who has the rest of the proverb
"Actions speak louder . . ."?

I have
losers weepers.

Who has the rest of the proverb
"It takes two to . . ."?

I Have, Who Has?: Language Arts • 5–6 © 2006 Creative Teaching Press

Proverbs

I have
tango.

Who has the rest of the proverb
"All work and no play
makes Jack . . ."?

I have
are free.

Who has the rest of the proverb
"Patience is a . . ."?

I have
a dull boy.

Who has the rest of the proverb
"Absence makes the . . ."?

I have
virtue.

Who has the rest of the proverb
"Practice makes . . ."?

I have
heart grow fonder.

Who has the rest of the proverb
"Two heads are better . . ."?

I have
perfect.

Who has the rest of the proverb
"Better late . . ."?

I have
than one.

Who has the rest of the proverb
"Beggars can't be . . ."?

I have
than never.

Who has the rest of the proverb
"Out of sight . . ."?

I have
choosers.

Who has the rest of the proverb
"The best things in life . . ."?

I have
out of mind

Who has the first card?

Proverbs

As your classmates identify the end of each proverb, lightly color in the matching box to uncover the hidden proverb and its meaning. Listen closely so you don't miss any answers.

FLOCK TOGETHER	SKIN DEEP	TANGO	EAT IT TOO	BOWL OF CHERRIES
NOTHING	THAN NEVER	MEDICINE	THAN ONE	GO ROUND
BEFORE THEY HATCH	ALL EVILS	MAKE A RIGHT	LOST	ARE FREE
VENTURED	MAY FLOWERS	NOTHING	CHOOSERS	VIRTUE
THE MICE WILL PLAY	OUT OF MIND	BELIEVING	GAINED	THERE IS A WAY
YOU LOSE SOME	IN THE MOUTH	MEANS THAT	THAN WORDS	IS BLISS
LEAP	YOU WILL NEVER	SORRY	SUCCEED	HEART GROW FONDER
A DULL BOY	ON THE OTHER SIDE OF THE FENCE	FAST	KEEPS THE DOCTOR AWAY	IN ANYTHING
PERFECT	UNLESS YOU	IS NOT GOLD	ARE WILLING	FRIEND INDEED
THINK ALIKE	TO TRY	WATER	HEAR NO LIES	LOSERS WEEPERS

Write the proverb and meaning you uncovered.

_____

_____

Describe in complete sentences a time when you realized that practice makes perfect.

_____

Describe in complete sentences what you think "it takes two to tango" means.

_____

I Have, Who Has?: Language Arts • 5–6 © 2006 Creative Teaching Press

I have the **first card.**

Who has something that fits these clues: *play, music, keys*?

I have **beach.**

Who has something that fits these clues: *retina, iris, lid*?

I have **piano.**

Who has something that fits these clues: *carbonated, drink, bubbles*?

I have **eye.**

Who has something that fits these clues: *chew, mouth, white*?

I have **soda.**

Who has something that fits these clues: *wheels, pedals, handlebars*?

I have **teeth.**

Who has something that fits these clues: *cumulus, rain, billowy*?

I have **bicycle.**

Who has something that fits these clues: *popped, cob, kernels*?

I have **clouds.**

Who has something that fits these clues: *books, school, carrier*?

I have **corn.**

Who has something that fits these clues: *sand, salt water, waves*?

I have **backpack.**

Who has something that fits these clues: *warmth, soft, feet*?

I have **socks.**

Who has something that fits these clues: *smell, blow, septum*?

I have **book.**

Who has something that fits these clues: *focus, lens, flash*?

I have **nose.**

Who has something that fits these clues: *vaults, money, tellers*?

I have **camera.**

Who has something that fits these clues: *sleep, soft, clothing*?

I have **bank.**

Who has something that fits these clues: *popcorn, movies, building*?

I have **pajamas.**

Who has something that fits these clues: *hands, wall, time*?

I have **theater.**

Who has something that fits these clues: *letter, postage, lick*?

I have **clock.**

Who has something that fits these clues: *den, mammal, grizzly*?

I have **stamp.**

Who has something that fits these clues: *pages, cover, title*?

I have **bear.**

Who has something that fits these clues: *fly, tickets, vehicle*?

I Have, Who Has?: Language Arts • 5–6 © 2006 Creative Teaching Press

Critical Thinking and Deduction 1

I have **plane.**

Who has something that fits these clues: *yellow, sour, fruit*?

I have **coffee.**

Who has something that fits these clues: *sticky, seal, wrapping*?

I have **lemon.**

Who has something that fits these clues: *ball, sport, racket*?

I have **tape.**

Who has something that fits these clues: *orange, rabbit, food*?

I have **tennis.**

Who has something that fits these clues: *clean, fresh, teeth*?

I have **carrot.**

Who has something that fits these clues: *apple, dessert, round*?

I have **toothpaste.**

Who has something that fits these clues: *electric, shade, bright*?

I have **pie.**

Who has something that fits these clues: *books, borrow, fine*?

I have **lamp.**

Who has something that fits these clues: *hot, cream and sugar, beverage*?

I have **library.**

Who has something that fits these clues: *croutons, healthy, green*?

I Have, Who Has?: Language Arts • 5–6 © 2006 Creative Teaching Press

Critical Thinking and Deduction 1

I have **salad.**

Who has something that fits these clues: *temperature, sick, fever*?

I have **ants.**

Who has something that fits these clues: *unlock, chain, door*?

I have **thermometer.**

Who has something that fits these clues: *heavy, boat, water*?

I have **key.**

Who has something that fits these clues: *cut, crafts, sharp*?

I have **anchor.**

Who has something that fits these clues: *peel, potassium, yellow*?

I have **scissors.**

Who has something that fits these clues: *permed, frizzy, grows*?

I have **banana.**

Who has something that fits these clues: *engine, track, cars*?

I have **hair.**

Who has something that fits these clues: *nest, fly, sing*?

I have **train.**

Who has something that fits these clues: *pests, black, picnic*?

I have **bird.**

Who has the first card?

I Have, Who Has?: Language Arts • 5–6 © 2006 Creative Teaching Press

Critical Thinking and Deduction 1

As your classmates identify each word, lightly color in the matching box. Listen closely so you don't miss any answers.

NOSE	LAMP	TEETH	STAMP	SOCKS
BANANA	CATALOG	TOOTHPASTE	ANIMAL	ANCHOR
EYE	THEATER	PIANO	TENNIS	HAIR
COFFEE	BOOK	TRAIN	RADIO	BACKPACK
NEEDLE	BEAR	THERMOMETER	CLOCK	IMAGINATION
BICYCLE	VIOLIN	CLOUDS	ORANGUTAN	SCISSORS
TAPE	LEMON	BIRD	PLANE	BANK
RABBIT	PAJAMAS	PIE	SODA	KEY
CORN	ORGAN	ANTS	CAMERA	LIBRARY
UMBRELLA	BEACH	SNAKE	CARROT	SALAD

Write the first letter of each word you did not color over. Go from left to right, beginning with the first row. What is the mystery word?

_____ _____ _____ _____ _____ _____ _____ _____ _____ _____

Write three clues that you could give a classmate about this word.

_____

_____

_____

Critical Thinking and Deduction 2

I have the **first card.**

Who has something that fits these clues: *time, hands, wrist?*

I have **apple.**

Who has something that fits these clues: *animal, hop, furry?*

I have **watch.**

Who has something that fits these clues: *mouse, monitor, e-mail?*

I have **bunny.**

Who has something that fits these clues: *batteries, camping, light?*

I have **computer.**

Who has something that fits these clues: *liquid, scent, women?*

I have **flashlight.**

Who has something that fits these clues: *snow, ski, season?*

I have **perfume.**

Who has something that fits these clues: *polo, saddle, mane?*

I have **winter.**

Who has something that fits these clues: *paper, coins, spend?*

I have **horse.**

Who has something that fits these clues: *red, doctor, core?*

I have **money.**

Who has something that fits these clues: *net, ball, court?*

I Have, Who Has?: Language Arts • 5–6 © 2006 Creative Teaching Press

I have **basketball.**

Who has something that fits these clues: *gem, famous city, green?*

I have **flag.**

Who has something that fits these clues: *dessert, frosting, candles?*

I have **emerald.**

Who has something that fits these clues: *sweet, queen, bees?*

I have **cake.**

Who has something that fits these clues: *leaves, roots, trunk?*

I have **honey.**

Who has something that fits these clues: *canvas, sleep, camping?*

I have **tree.**

Who has something that fits these clues: *artist, wall, hang?*

I have **tent.**

Who has something that fits these clues: *eraser, write, lead?*

I have **painting.**

Who has something that fits these clues: *man, throne, rule?*

I have **pencil.**

Who has something that fits these clues: *stripes, symbol, stars?*

I have **king.**

Who has something that fits these clues: *cruise, vehicle, ocean?*

I have **yacht.**

Who has something that fits these clues: *leader, elected, White House?*

I have **castle.**

Who has something that fits these clues: *ball, pins, alley?*

I have **President.**

Who has something that fits these clues: *mountain, dangerous, lava?*

I have **bowling.**

Who has something that fits these clues: *animal, hump, desert?*

I have **volcano.**

Who has something that fits these clues: *pump, blood, organ?*

I have **camel.**

Who has something that fits these clues: *answer, ring tones, text message?*

I have **heart.**

Who has something that fits these clues: *chicken, yolk, scrambled?*

I have **cell phone.**

Who has something that fits these clues: *hard, frozen, melts?*

I have **eggs.**

Who has something that fits these clues: *moat, home, queen?*

I have **ice.**

Who has something that fits these clues: *utensil, eat, prongs?*

I Have, Who Has?: Language Arts • 5–6 © 2006 Creative Teaching Press

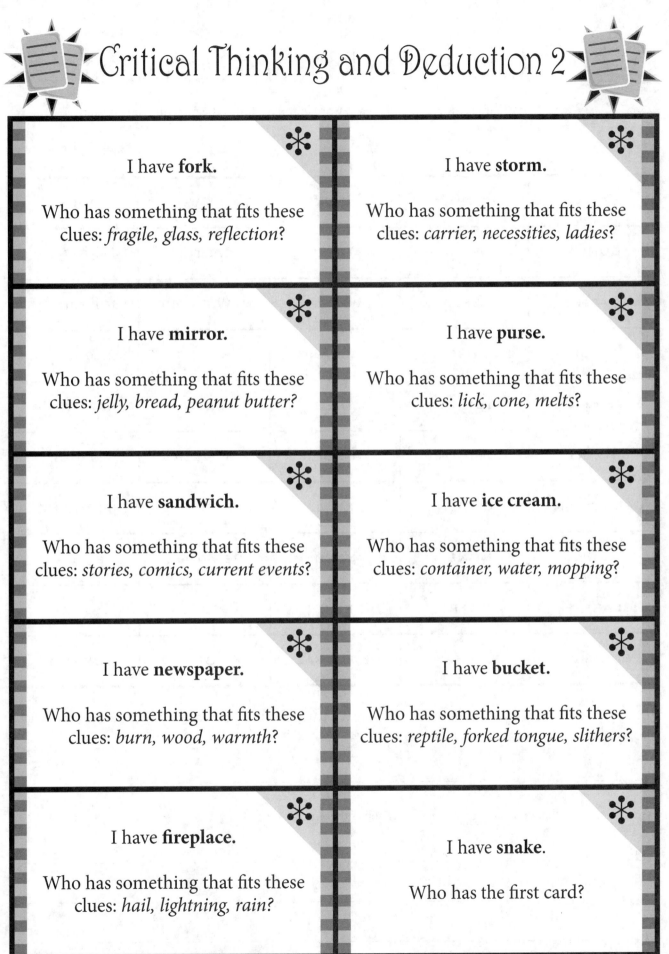

I have **fork.**

Who has something that fits these clues: *fragile, glass, reflection?*

I have **storm.**

Who has something that fits these clues: *carrier, necessities, ladies?*

I have **mirror.**

Who has something that fits these clues: *jelly, bread, peanut butter?*

I have **purse.**

Who has something that fits these clues: *lick, cone, melts?*

I have **sandwich.**

Who has something that fits these clues: *stories, comics, current events?*

I have **ice cream.**

Who has something that fits these clues: *container, water, mopping?*

I have **newspaper.**

Who has something that fits these clues: *burn, wood, warmth?*

I have **bucket.**

Who has something that fits these clues: *reptile, forked tongue, slithers?*

I have **fireplace.**

Who has something that fits these clues: *hail, lightning, rain?*

I have **snake.**

Who has the first card?

I Have, Who Has?: Language Arts • 5–6 © 2006 Creative Teaching Press

Critical Thinking and Deduction 2

As your classmates identify each word, lightly color in the matching box. Listen closely so you don't miss any answers.

PENCIL	PRESIDENT	TENT	FLAG	PURSE
BUNNY	BOWLING	MANDIBLE	CASTLE	APPLE
YACHT	FIREPLACE	WATCH	NEWSPAPER	ICE CREAM
ONION	CAMEL	VOLCANO	HONEY	CAKE
FLASHLIGHT	TURNIP	TREE	OXEN	SANDWICH
SNAKE	COMPUTER	RUBBER	WINTER	EGGS
CELL PHONE	CLOWN	KING	MIRROR	PAINTING
HORSE	MONEY	YOLK	PERFUME	BUCKET
CLARINET	HEART	LEMUR	ICE	STORM
EMERALD	ELEPHANT	BASKETBALL	FORK	SURPRISE

Write the first letter of each word you did not color over. Go from left to right, beginning with the first row. What is the mystery word?

_____ _ _____ _____ _____ _____ _____ _____ _____ _____

Write three clues that you could give a classmate about this word.

_____

_____

_____

I Have, Who Has?: Language Arts • 5–6 © 2006 Creative Teaching Press

Oxymorons

I have the **first card.**

Who has the oxymoron that matches this clue: icy cold place on fire?

I have **power nap.**

Who has the oxymoron that matches this clue: not short and clothing worn above the knees?

I have **freezer burn.**

Who has the oxymoron that matches this clue: dark color brightness?

I have **long shorts.**

Who has the oxymoron that matches this clue: pointy bends?

I have **black light.**

Who has the oxymoron that matches this clue: put yourself in a chair and the opposite of *down*?

I have **sharp curves.**

Who has the oxymoron that matches this clue: tasty treat without sugar?

I have **sit up.**

Who has the oxymoron that matches this clue: truthful person fibbing?

I have **sugarless candy.**

Who has the oxymoron that matches this clue: relaxed and rainy weather condition?

I have **honest liar.**

Who has the oxymoron that matches this clue: energy rest?

I have **calm storm.**

Who has the oxymoron that matches this clue: noisy quiet talk?

Oxymorons

I have
loud whisper.

Who has the oxymoron that matches this clue: absolutely incorrect?

I have
old news.

Who has the oxymoron that matches this clue: seasonal education?

I have
positively wrong.

Who has the oxymoron that matches this clue: smallest amount and most popular?

I have
summer school.

Who has the oxymoron that matches this clue: bending unending rays?

I have
least favorite.

Who has the oxymoron that matches this clue: absolutely silly?

I have
curved lines.

Who has the oxymoron that matches this clue: cruel happy look?

I have
perfectly ridiculous.

Who has the oxymoron that matches this clue: small disaster?

I have
mean smile.

Who has the oxymoron that matches this clue: not ever repeated?

I have
minor catastrophe.

Who has the oxymoron that matches this clue: ancient information?

I have
never again.

Who has the oxymoron that matches this clue: not seen writing liquid?

I Have, Who Has?: Language Arts • 5–6 © 2006 Creative Teaching Press

Oxymorons

I have **invisible ink.**

Who has the oxymoron that matches this clue: unique duplicate?

I have **home office.**

Who has the oxymoron that matches this clue: single option?

I have **original copy.**

Who has the oxymoron that matches this clue: obviously confused?

I have **one choice.**

Who has the oxymoron that matches this clue: entire section?

I have **clearly misunderstood.**

Who has the oxymoron that matches this clue: unhappy circus performer?

I have **whole piece.**

Who has the oxymoron that matches this clue: huge little shellfish?

I have **sad clown.**

Who has the oxymoron that matches this clue: sleeping celebration?

I have **jumbo shrimp.**

Who has the oxymoron that matches this clue: not tight method of tying rope?

I have **slumber party.**

Who has the oxymoron that matches this clue: house workplace?

I have **loose knot.**

Who has the oxymoron that matches this clue: not outside in?

I Have, Who Has?: Language Arts • 5–6 © 2006 Creative Teaching Press

Oxymorons

I have
inside out.

Who has the oxymoron that matches this clue: awfully adorable?

I have
small fortune.

Who has the oxymoron that matches this clue: not humorous playtime?

I have
terribly cute.

Who has the oxymoron that matches this clue: showed up and gone?

I have
serious fun.

Who has the oxymoron that matches this clue: neat and tidy confusion?

I have
turned up missing.

Who has the oxymoron that matches this clue: quiet warning noise?

I have
organized chaos.

Who has the oxymoron that matches this clue: perform without faking?

I have
silent alarm.

Who has the oxymoron that matches this clue: not wet frozen water?

I have
act naturally.

Who has the oxymoron that matches this clue: opposite of hot perspiration?

I have
dry ice.

Who has the oxymoron that matches this clue: tiny vast amount of money?

I have
cold sweat.

Who has the first card?

I Have, Who Has?: Language Arts • 5–6 © 2006 Creative Teaching Press

Oxymorons

As your classmates identify each oxymoron, lightly color in the matching box to uncover the hidden oxymoron and explanation. Listen closely so you don't miss any answers.

WHOLE PIECE	PEOPLE WHO	LOUD WHISPER	DON'T LIKE	JUMBO SHRIMP
SIT UP	LEAST FAVORITE	WAKING UP	MEAN SMILE	POSITIVELY WRONG
SUMMER SCHOOL	COLD SWEAT	FREEZER BURN	SILENT ALARM	INVISIBLE INK
DRY ICE	CALM STORM	IN THE MORNING	CURVED LINES	ONE CHOICE
SAY THAT	HOME OFFICE	PERFECTLY RIDICULOUS	ACT NATURALLY	SUGARLESS CANDY
BLACK LIGHT	TURNED UP MISSING	THE	NEVER AGAIN	PHRASE
SAD CLOWN	ORGANIZED CHAOS	HONEST LIAR	SMALL FORTUNE	LOOSE KNOT
"GOOD MORNING"	MINOR CATASTROPHE	IS	OLD NEWS	SHARP CURVES
LONG SHORTS	AN	INSIDE OUT	SERIOUS FUN	TERRIBLY CUTE
SLUMBER PARTY	CLEARLY MISUNDERSTOOD	OXYMORON	POWER NAP	ORIGINAL COPY

Write the oxymoron and explanation you uncovered.

_____

Why would people say that? Explain your answer in a complete sentence.

_____

Why do some people think the term "mild jalapeño" is an oxymoron?

_____

Associative Connections 1

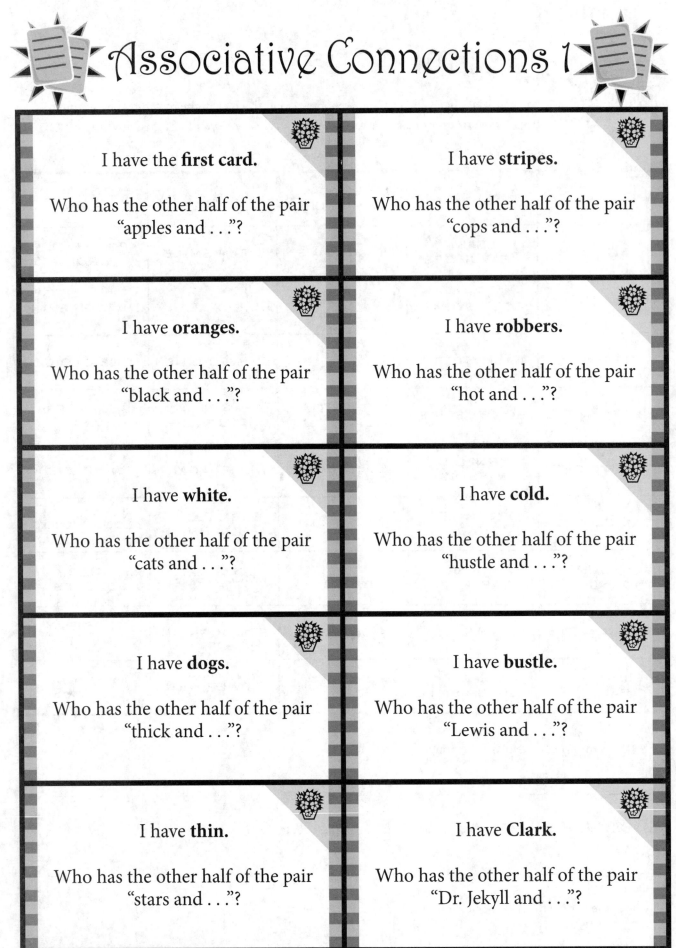

I have the **first card.**

Who has the other half of the pair "apples and . . ."?

I have **stripes.**

Who has the other half of the pair "cops and . . ."?

I have **oranges.**

Who has the other half of the pair "black and . . ."?

I have **robbers.**

Who has the other half of the pair "hot and . . ."?

I have **white.**

Who has the other half of the pair "cats and . . ."?

I have **cold.**

Who has the other half of the pair "hustle and . . ."?

I have **dogs.**

Who has the other half of the pair "thick and . . ."?

I have **bustle.**

Who has the other half of the pair "Lewis and . . ."?

I have **thin.**

Who has the other half of the pair "stars and . . ."?

I have **Clark.**

Who has the other half of the pair "Dr. Jekyll and . . ."?

I Have, Who Has?: Language Arts • 5–6 © 2006 Creative Teaching Press

Associative Connections 1

I have **Mr. Hyde.**

Who has the other half of the pair "green eggs and . . ."?

I have **democrat.**

Who has the other half of the pair "Senate and . . ."?

I have **ham.**

Who has the other half of the pair "lost and . . ."?

I have **House of Representatives.**

Who has the other half of the pair "toss and . . ."?

I have **found.**

Who has the other half of the pair "rock and . . ."?

I have **turn.**

Who has the other half of the pair "credit and . . ."?

I have **roll.**

Who has the other half of the pair "cream and . . ."?

I have **debit.**

Who has the other half of the pair "east and . . ."?

I have **sugar.**

Who has the other half of the pair "republican and . . ."?

I have **west.**

Who has the other half of the pair "north and . . ."?

Associative Connections 1

I have **south.**

Who has the other half of the pair "compare and . . ."?

I have **rescue.**

Who has the other half of the pair "meat and . . ."?

I have **contrast.**

Who has the other half of the pair "above and . . ."?

I have **potatoes**.

Who has the other half of the pair "odd and . . ."?

I have **beyond.**

Who has the other half of the pair "forgive and . . ."?

I have **even.**

Who has the other half of the pair "bat and . . ."?

I have **forget.**

Who has the other half of the pair "once and . . ."?

I have **ball.**

Who has the other half of the pair "shoes and . . ."?

I have **for all.**

Who has the other half of the pair "search and . . ."?

I have **socks.**

Who has the other half of the pair "rich and . . ."?

I Have, Who Has?: Language Arts • 5–6 © 2006 Creative Teaching Press

Associative Connections 1

I have **famous.**

Who has the other half of the pair "flora and . . ."?

I have **pepper.**

Who has the other half of the pair "left and . . ."?

I have **fauna.**

Who has the other half of the pair "dollars and . . ."?

I have **right.**

Who has the other half of the pair "fair and . . ."?

I have **cents.**

Who has the other half of the pair "cause and . . ."?

I have **square.**

Who has the other half of the pair "bagels and . . ."?

I have **effect.**

Who has the other half of the pair "enter and . . ."?

I have **cream cheese.**

Who has the other half of the pair "cups and . . . "?

I have **exit.**

Who has the other half of the pair "salt and . . ."?

I have **saucers.**

Who has the first card?

I Have, Who Has? Language Arts • 5–6 © 2006 Creative Teaching Press

Associative Connections 1

As your classmates identify each paired word, lightly color in the matching box. Listen closely so you don't miss any answers.

WHITE	BANDANA	DOGS	EXIT	TURN
ROLL	CONTRAST	ORANGES	CLARK	RACECAR
POTATOES	RESCUE	FOR ALL	FORGET	BEYOND
SUGAR	MR. HYDE	EAGLE	HOUSE OF REPRESENTATIVES	ARMY
DREAM	THIN	EFFECT	BUSTLE	CENTS
FAUNA	PEPPER	SOUTH	CREAM CHEESE	HAM
DEMOCRAT	STRIPES	BADMINTON	FOUND	UMPIRE
BALL	TAXES	EVEN	SQUARE	DEBIT
ROBBERS	FAMOUS	RIGHT	COLD	TIRE
ENVELOPE	WEST	RAINCOAT	SOCKS	SAUCERS

Write the first letter of each word you did not color over. Go from left to right, beginning with the first row. What is the pair of mystery words?

_____ _____ _____ _____ _____ and _____ _____ _____ _____ _____ _____

List three more familiar word pairs that are not part of the game.

_____

_____

_____

I Have, Who Has?: Language Arts • 5–6 © 2006 Creative Teaching Press

Associative Connections 2

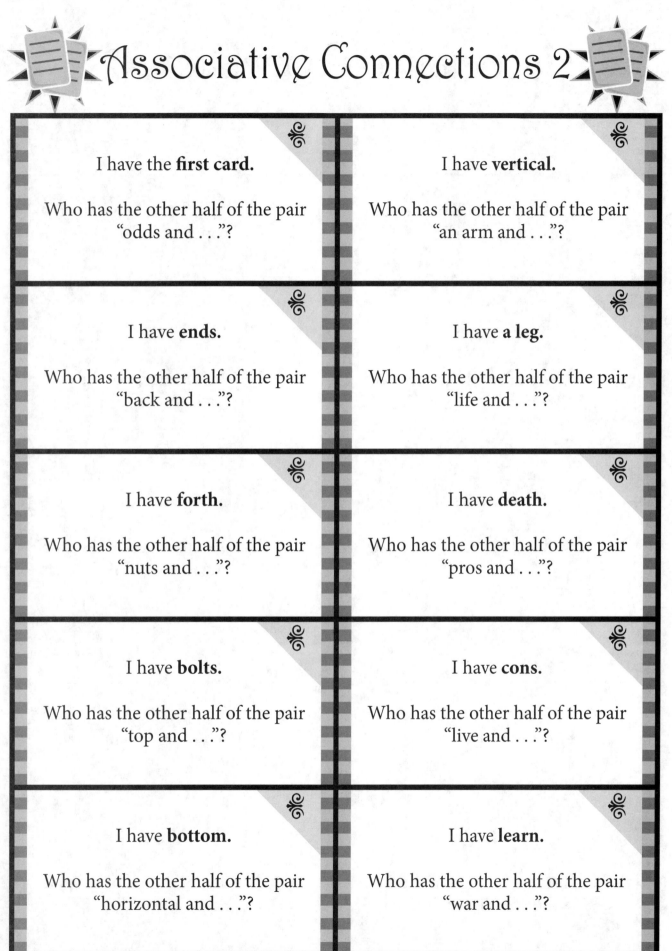

I have the **first card.**

Who has the other half of the pair "odds and . . ."?

I have **vertical.**

Who has the other half of the pair "an arm and . . ."?

I have **ends.**

Who has the other half of the pair "back and . . ."?

I have **a leg.**

Who has the other half of the pair "life and . . ."?

I have **forth.**

Who has the other half of the pair "nuts and . . ."?

I have **death.**

Who has the other half of the pair "pros and . . ."?

I have **bolts.**

Who has the other half of the pair "top and . . ."?

I have **cons.**

Who has the other half of the pair "live and . . ."?

I have **bottom.**

Who has the other half of the pair "horizontal and . . ."?

I have **learn.**

Who has the other half of the pair "war and . . ."?

I Have, Who Has?: Language Arts • 5–6 © 2006 Creative Teaching Press

Associative Connections 2

I have **peace.**

Who has the other half of the pair "soap and . . ."?

I have **lightning.**

Who has the other half of the pair "paper and . . ."?

I have **water.**

Who has the other half of the pair "winners and . . ."?

I have **pencil.**

Who has the other half of the pair "safe and . . ."?

I have **losers.**

Who has the other half of the pair "pins and . . ."?

I have **sound.**

Who has the other half of the pair "sugar and . . ."?

I have **needles.**

Who has the other half of the pair "Hansel and . . ."?

I have **spice.**

Who has the other half of the pair "Pocahontas and . . ."?

I have **Gretel.**

Who has the other half of the pair "thunder and . . ."?

I have **John Smith.**

Who has the other half of the pair "right and . . ."?

I Have, Who Has?: Language Arts • 5–6 © 2006 Creative Teaching Press

Associative Connections 2

I have **wrong.**

Who has the other half of the pair "head and . . ."?

I have **Robin.**

Who has the other half of the pair "cheese and . . ."?

I have **shoulders.**

Who has the other half of the pair "scratch and . . ."?

I have **crackers.**

Who has the other half of the pair "peanut butter and . . ."?

I have **sniff.**

Who has the other half of the pair "biscuits and . . ."?

I have **jelly.**

Who has the other half of the pair "ladies and . . ."?

I have **gravy.**

Who has the other half of the pair "show and . . ."?

I have **gentlemen.**

Who has the other half of the pair "shampoo and . . ."?

I have **tell.**

Who has the other half of the pair "Batman and . . ."?

I have **conditioner.**

Who has the other half of the pair "bread and . . ."?

I Have, Who Has?: Language Arts • 5–6 © 2006 Creative Teaching Press

I have **butter.**

Who has the other half of the pair "sticks and . . ."?

I have **thank you.**

Who has the other half of the pair "true and . . ."?

I have **stones.**

Who has the other half of the pair "spaghetti and . . ."?

I have **false.**

Who has the other half of the pair "bright and . . ."?

I have **meatballs.**

Who has the other half of the pair "black and . . ."?

I have **early.**

Who has the other half of the pair "buy and . . ."?

I have **blue.**

Who has the other half of the pair "tried and . . ."?

I have **sell.**

Who has the other half of the pair "profit and . . ."?

I have **true.**

Who has the other half of the pair "please and . . ."?

I have **loss.**

Who has the first card?

I Have, Who Has?: Language Arts • 5–6 © 2006 Creative Teaching Press

Associative Connections 2

As your classmates identify each paired word, lightly color in the matching box. Listen closely so you don't miss any answers.

John Smith	COCKROACH	SOUND	TRUE	GRAVY
BLUE	DEATH	LADYBUG	ENDS	SELL
SPICE	BUTTER	CONS	THANK YOU	PENCIL
LOSERS	ONION	SNIFF	TELL	LEARN
SHOULDERS	FORTH	CONDITIONER	STONES	PEACE
GENTLEMEN	APPLE	LIGHTNING	A LEG	WATER
KANGAROO	VERTICAL	DOG	MEATBALLS	LOSS
NEEDLES	WRONG	APE	BOLTS	FALSE
GARDEN	GRAPES	ROBIN	GRETEL	CRACKERS
JELLY	BOTTOM	EMU	ROOSTER	EARLY

Write the first letter of each word you did not color over. Go from left to right, beginning with the first row. What is the pair of mystery words?

_____ _____ _____ _____ _____ and _____ _____ _____ _____ _____ _____

List three more familiar word pairs that are not part of the game.

_____

_____

_____

I Have, Who Has?: Language Arts • 5–6 © 2006 Creative Teaching Press

Clichés

I have the **first card.**

Who has the rest of the cliché "Never say …"?

I have **on eggshells.**

Who has the rest of the cliché "He's skating on …"?

I have **never.**

Who has the rest of the cliché "One size …"?

I have **thin ice.**

Who has the rest of the cliché "I have a frog in …"?

I have **fits all.**

Who has the rest of the cliché "The third time's …"?

I have **my throat.**

Who has the rest of the cliché "This is the greatest thing …"?

I have **the charm.**

Who has the rest of the cliché "It's only a matter …"?

I have **since sliced bread.**

Who has the rest of the cliché "This is the cream …"?

I have **of time.**

Who has the rest of the cliché "It's like walking …"?

I have **of the crop.**

Who has the rest of the cliché "If the shoe fits …"?

I Have, Who Has?: Language Arts • 5–6 © 2006 Creative Teaching Press

Clichés

I have **wear it.**

Who has the rest of the cliché "That's right up …"?

I have **the draw.**

Who has the rest of the cliché "This is not my …"?

I have **your alley.**

Who has the rest of the cliché "Now the tables …"?

I have **cup of tea.**

Who has the rest of the cliché "We're taking the scenic …"?

I have **are turned.**

Who has the rest of the cliché "The sky's …"?

I have **route.**

Who has the rest of the cliché "I'll turn over …"?

I have **the limit.**

Who has the rest of the cliché "He's playing with…"?

I have **a new leaf.**

Who has the rest of the cliché "It's mind over …"?

I have **fire.**

Who has the rest of the cliché "That's the luck of …"?

I have **matter.**

Who has the rest of the cliché "She's down to …"?

I Have, Who Has?: Language Arts • 5–6 © 2006 Creative Teaching Press

Clichés

I have **earth.**

Who has the rest of the cliché "We've got it made in the …"?

I have **a star.**

Who has the rest of the cliché "It costs a pretty …"?

I have **shade.**

Who has the rest of the cliché "I'm saved by …"?

I have **penny.**

Who has the rest of the cliché "You're the apple of my …"?

I have **the bell.**

Who has the rest of the cliché "It's an open and shut …"?

I have **eye.**

Who has the rest of the cliché "Bite your …"?

I have **case.**

Who has the rest of the cliché "He'll roll over in …"?

I have **tongue.**

Who has the rest of the cliché "Knock yourself …"?

I have **his grave.**

Who has the rest of the cliché "I'll wish upon …"?

I have **out.**

Who has the rest of the cliché "Turn the …"?

I Have, Who Has?: Language Arts • 5–6 © 2006 Creative Teaching Press

Clichés

I have **other cheek.**

Who has the rest of the cliché
"You're just twiddling your …"?

I have **tree.**

Who has the rest of the cliché
"I missed it …"?

I have **thumbs.**

Who has the rest of the cliché
"She fell head over …"?

I have **by a hair.**

Who has the rest of the cliché
"This is my ace
in the …"?

I have **heels.**

Who has the rest of the cliché
"That was a stroke of good …"?

I have **hole.**

Who has the rest of the cliché
"Don't rock the …"?

I have **luck.**

Who has the rest of the cliché
"Put a cork …"?

I have **boat.**

Who has the rest of the cliché
"That'll be the …"?

I have **in it.**

Who has the rest of the cliché
"You're barking up the wrong …"?

I have **day.**

Who has the first card?

Clichés

As your classmates identify each cliché, lightly color in the matching box to uncover the hidden cliché and its meaning. Listen closely so you don't miss any answers.

TONGUE	YOUR ALLEY	PULL A	NEVER	LUCK
THE LIMIT	IN IT	ARE TURNED	OUT	THE DRAW
FAST	SHADE	ONE	EARTH	HEELS
MY THROAT	A NEW LEAF	FITS ALL	MEANS	FIRE
THAT	EYE	TREE	ON EGGSHELLS	OTHER CHEEK
MATTER	ROUTE	PENNY	OF TIME	A PERSON
TRIES TO	THIN ICE	DAY	THE CHARM	CUP OF TEA
WEAR IT	TRICK	THE BELL	THUMBS	AND
DOUBLE-CROSS	OF THE CROP	BY A HAIR	HIS GRAVE	SINCE SLICED BREAD
A STAR	SOMEONE	CASE	HOLE	BOAT

Write the cliché and meaning you uncovered.

_____

Explain the cliché "time flies when you're having fun" in complete sentences.

_____

Explain the cliché "cool as a cucumber" in complete sentences.

_____

I Have, Who Has?: Language Arts • 5–6 © 2006 Creative Teaching Press

Answer Key

Synonyms 1 (Page 10)

TRY	A	FOOLISH	TASTY	OFTEN
DISTURB	CRISIS	LOUD	IMITATE	SHY
MAKE	LEAVE	PENNY	PLAIN	SAVED
IS	SLUGGISH	SHOW	ATTRACTIVE	VIEWPOINT
JOYFUL	HUGE	A PENNY	TARDY	ITEM
INFAMOUS	DESCRIBE	FAMISHED	LUCKY	JOB
RUSH	EARNED	CLOTHED	ERROR	COMPREHEND
CONCEAL	FATAL	CURRENT	AID	SUDDEN
FIND	REST	PIECE	EDUCATE	HONEST

Possible synonyms for *saved*: collected, accumulated, gathered
Possible synonyms for *earned*: received, made

Synonyms 2 (Page 15)

AWFUL	EASY	SMELL	HELP	TRY
PLEDGE	RECALL	GRIEF	SHAKE	BRAVE
MIX	SPARKLING	CHOOSE	FINISH	LEAVE
WARN	DESTROY	CLOTHING	IMMENSE	MATCHING
AN APPLE	STRANGE	BEG	THICK	MEND
RULE	A DAY	BUY	SCARED	BEGIN
WEARY	VANISH	DAMP	RESPOND	HILARIOUS
KEEPS	SMART	WANT	JUMP	CLOSE
THE	HURT	DOCTOR	ALLY	AWAY

Possible synonyms for *keeps*: holds back, maintains
Answers will vary.

Synonyms 3 (Page 20)

FRAGILE	COPY	PART	OBTAIN	EVENT
FLAW	CHOOSE	BEND	DEPRESSION	BRAVE
PAIR	NOISELESS	BUY	DISCUSS	TIME
LEAVE	HEALS	CONTAMINATED	WORRY	FEAST
ALL	ACHIEVE	HARM	TIMID	BUILD
BRAG	DELAY	AIDE	WOUNDS	POLITE
WEALTHY	EXCUSE	TRICK	FAKE	TRIP
THINK	REACH	COLLECT	GENUINE	ORDER
DECREASE	SHRIEK	ARGUE	.	.

Possible synonyms for *heals*: cures, soothes, fixes, mends, repairs
Possible synonyms for *wounds*: injuries, cuts, sores

Synonyms 4 (Page 25)

GRATITUDE	DESTROY	VERDICT	ODD	FRIEND
RAW	EXOTIC	END	TREK	CHOICE
BEAUTY	FEELINGS	GLOOMY	ESSENTIAL	ENJOY
FUNNY	IS	PROBLEM	CLAIM	GIGANTIC
ONLY	STRONG	SKIN	FIX	PREDICT
SCAN	DEEP	PLAIN	VISIBLE	FIND
SICKNESS	FRAGILE	NERVOUS	AGED	PERSIST
LEAVE	CHEAP	HIRE	FREEDOM	WONDERFUL
CONSTRUCTIVE	FALSE	FAIRNESS	DANGEROUS	.

Possible synonyms for *beauty*: looks, appearance
Possible synonyms for *deep*: thick, broad

Antonyms 1 (Page 30)

OPEN	WRONG	FORWARD	SINK	COUNTER-CLOCKWISE
WILT	MORNING	PLAY	NOTICE	STURDY
WEAK	DISHONEST	SIMILAR	BORED	LOSE
SAFE	MISPLACE	GREEDY	DON'T	DAMAGE
PLEASANT	PUT ALL	WRAP	YOUR	PATIENT
EGGS	FALL	IN ONE	ENDING	URGENT
SEND	BASKET	DEMOCRAT	MALE	SELL
DESPISED	SYNTHETIC	EXPORT	NERVOUS	OWE
UNLIKELY	DESOLATE	LATE	EXPIRED	HUMID

Possible antonyms for *put*: take away, remove
Possible antonyms for *in*: out, outside

Antonyms 2 (Page 35)

OPEN	FIRST	EXPENSE	INFERIOR	CALM
TIRED	FIND	A FOOL	CATCH	REWARD
CLARIFY	FOE	AGREE	LIGHT	RESPONSIBLE
CLIMB	AND HIS	RUDE	PROTECT	DEPART
FULL	PAST	ALLOW	ADD	MONEY
ARE	READY	EXIT	SOON	ANTONYM
PUBLIC	SUPPORT	PARTED	COMBINE	FAIR
TINY	DIVIDE	MESSY	CRY	VERTEBRATE
THANKFUL	PACK	BALD	HUMBLE	MISERY

Possible antonyms for *fool*: genius, master
Possible antonyms for *parted*: joined, connected

Antonyms 3 (Page 40)

TARDY	LEND	WEST	GUILTY	PERMANENT
WARMED	DESTROY	SOLID	MONEY	FINISH
IS	ACCEPT	AWAKE	CLEAN	THE
STRANGE	COSTLY	ROOT	ELDERLY	TAKE
FALL	WIDE	SUCCESS	WILD	POOR
ANSWER	ILL	WINTER	OF ALL	NOISE
FULL	BORING	EVIL	TRAP	GROW
SIMPLE	NEGATIVE	CONNECT	ODD	REST
TIGHT	INSULT	TRUE	COURTEOUS	FACT

Possible antonyms for *root*: result, ending
Possible antonyms for *evil*: goodness, benevolence

Antonyms 4 (Page 45)

HONESTY	DRY	PRESENT	DEFEAT	IS
STALE	FORGET	CHEERFUL	THE	LOST
BEST	PROUD	CROOKED	PLAIN	DEFINITE
FLAVORLESS	HARD	PESSIMISTIC	SCARCE	MODERN
NOISY	CLEAR	LIGHT	POLICY	PERMIT
PART	SMILE	ALWAYS	ROUGH	DEEP
RIGHT	AFTER	SAVE	DELAY	JOIN
COMMON	RECKLESS	FOOLISH	FREEZE	OMIT
SUNNY	KIND	DOUBT	THIN	.

Possible antonyms for *honesty*: dishonesty, corruption
Possible antonyms for *best*: worst, most awful

Contractions 1 (Page 50)

WE'VE	WHO'LL	SHOULDN'T	THEY'VE	LOOK
HE'D	WOULDN'T	BEFORE	I'VE	THEY'LL
I'M	WHAT'S	IT'S	THAT'S	YOU'RE
YOU	LEAP	WE'RE	HOW'S	CAN'T
DOESN'T	WE'LL	I'LL	WOULD'VE	THEY'RE
DON'T	I'D	DIDN'T	HADN'T	COULDN'T
YOU'LL	AREN'T	YOU'VE	SHE'S	WHO'S
WASN'T	HE'S	YOU'D	SHOULD'VE	COULD'VE
WHAT'LL	WON'T	THEY'D	.	.

Possible answer: The proverb means that you should plan ahead before doing something.
Sentences will vary.

Contractions 2 (Page 55)

IN	YOU'D	WHAT'S	SHOULDN'T	ONE
WHO'S	SHE'D	WOULDN'T	DON'T	HE'D
WEREN'T	EAR	THEY'D	AND OUT	I'D
WHO'D	WHAT'LL	I'LL	WHEN'S	THE
WHERE'S	I'M	LET'S	IT'S	ISN'T
WE'D	SHE'LL	HE'S	HOW'S	HADN'T
OTHER	HASN'T	THAT'LL	THEY'VE	HAVEN'T
IT'LL	THERE'S	HERE'S	WON'T	THEY'RE
WE'LL	COULDN'T	AREN'T	WE'RE	THEY'LL

Sentences will vary.

Contractions 3 (Page 60)

SHE WOULD	ARE NOT	SHE IS	THEY WILL	WE HAVE
THERE	COULD NOT	IS NO	WOULD NOT	PLACE
HE WILL	LIKE	LET US	HOME	WAS NOT
IT WILL	THEY HAVE	I WOULD	YOU ARE	SHOULD NOT
CAN NOT	SHE WILL	WHO WILL	WE ARE	IS NOT
HAD NOT	DID NOT	WILL NOT	HAVE NOT	HE WOULD
IT IS	DO NOT	HE IS	I HAVE	DOES NOT
THEY ARE	WE WILL	HAS NOT	WERE NOT	I AM
COULD HAVE	I WILL	YOU WILL	YOU HAVE	*

Sentences will vary.

Details to the Main Idea 1 (Page 65)

THINGS USED FOR DRAWING	LOUD SOUNDS	EVEN NUMBERS	THINGS THAT COME IN THE MAIL	THINGS THAT ARE ROUND
COLD THINGS	VEGETABLES	THE GRASS	RED THINGS	IS ALWAYS
CONTINENTS	MONTHS	TYPES OF GROUND TRANSPORTATION	HEAVY THINGS	COUNTRIES IN EUROPE
SPORTS	FRUIT	YELLOW THINGS	TREES	RELATIVES
LANGUAGES	ANIMALS THAT HOP	GREENER	ON THE OTHER SIDE	THINGS WORN ON YOUR FEET
WEATHER	OF THE	BEVERAGES	DOGS	MEAL TIMES
FARM ANIMALS	FENCE	FISH	COINS	BODY PARTS
FORMS OF TRANSPORTATION	FLOWERS	GREEN THINGS	JEWELRY	THINGS THAT GIVE LIGHT
KITCHEN APPLIANCES	COLORS	U.S. PRESIDENTS	LINEAR SHAPES	THINGS THAT STRETCH

Answers will vary. Possible answers include:
pets—hamsters, rabbits, cats
state capitals—Montgomery, Juneau, Phoenix
school supplies—pencils, paper, ruler
beach—sand, ocean, waves

Details to the Main Idea 2 (Page 70)

FLOWERS	ABSENCE	RIVERS	MAKES	FRUIT
THE	ICE-CREAM FLAVORS	FACE PARTS	THINGS THAT TURN	TYPES OF MUSIC
CEREAL	RESTAURANT	HEART	PLANETS	UTENSILS
THINGS THAT CUT	OCEANS	BIRDS	CLOTHING	SENSES
NUTS	LANGUAGES	FEELINGS	STATES	ROOMS IN A HOUSE
MAJOR CITIES	GROW	PARTS OF A CAR	VEGETABLES	CHEESES
THINGS TO RECYCLE	TEXTURE WORDS	MUSICAL INSTRUMENTS	FLYING INSECTS	MEATS
SOUND WORDS	FABRICS	WEATHER FORECAST TERMS	THINGS FROM HAWAII	FAST THINGS
BLACK THINGS	TOOLS	THINGS ON AN AIRPLANE	BIRTHDAY PARTY	FONDER

Answers will vary. Possible answers include:
beverages—tea, juice, water
floor coverings—wood, carpet, tile
salty snacks—chips, pretzels, peanuts
school subjects— math, science, history

Main Idea to Details 1 (Page 75)

CARROTS, ASPARAGUS, KALE	TURKEY, PORK, BEEF	JAGUARS, PUMAS, LEOPARDS	ADJECTIVES, VERBS, CONJUNCTIONS	BROCCOLI, CAULIFLOWER, CELERY
FALL, SUMMER, SPRING	AFRICA, EUROPE, ASIA	TENNIS, GOLF, VOLLEYBALL	ONIONS, ENDIVE, CORN	ANGRY, SAD, HAPPY
CHEESE, SAUSAGE, PEPPERONI	STAPLER, PAPER CLIPS, PEN	CIRCLE, HEXAGON, TRIANGLE	THERMOMETER, BED, NURSE	TIRES, BALLOONS, RUBBER BALLS
BLENDER, IRON, COFFEEMAKER	BRUSH, HAIR DRYER, COMB	LATIN, FARSI, GREEK	PIGS, GOATS, TRACTOR	COFFEE, TEA, JUICE
BEANS, PEAS, SPROUTS	GULLS, EAGLES, OWLS	LIVING ROOM, OFFICE, DEN	OHIO, IDAHO, HAWAII	SODA, ICE, ARCTIC
E-MAIL, LETTERS, TELEPHONE CALLS	DUSTING, BEDMAKING, SWEEPING	SHELLS, TOWELS, SAND	STAMEN, ROOT, FLOWER	POPCORN, SODA, MOVIE
LETTUCE, MUSHROOMS, CILANTRO	SCREWDRIVER, SAW, HAMMER	LIMOUSINE, TRUCK, VAN	FEMUR, TIBIA, FIBULA	FIFTEEN, NINE, SEVEN
LIVER, SPLEEN, HEART	SPINACH, RADISH, GINGER	SPHERE, CONE, PYRAMID	CHECKERS, CHESS, CARDS	POLKA, SQUARE, TAP
TROMBONE, FLUTE, DRUMS	TULIP, DAISY, ROSE	LOLLIPOPS, JAWBREAKERS, LICORICE	CHINA, BRAZIL, CANADA	DESKS, RULER, PAPER

Possible categories for leftover words:
vegetables, healthy foods, foods that provide
vitamins or nourishment
Other items that fit the category: squash,
cucumber, tomato, eggplant

Main Idea to Details 2 (Page 80)

MOUSE, KEYBOARD, MONITOR	LIVER, ASPARAGUS, BROCCOLI	OCTOBER, MAY, MARCH	PAPER TOWELS, SPONGES, WASHCLOTHS	TEA, JUICE, WATER
TRACTORS, BULLDOZERS, WOOD	EAGLE, WOODPECKER, GULL	OLD FOOD, BROKEN GLASS, RINDS	CROUTONS, CARROTS, LETTUCE	BUS, SNAKE, MOSQUITO
SLIME, MUD, MELTED MARSHMALLOWS	HARES, KANGAROOS, GRASSHOPPERS	CHESS, HIDE-AND-SEEK, TAG	CHINESE WRITING, PLAYING SOCCER, LEARNING MULTIPLICATION	PRETZELS, CHIPS, CRACKERS
PLANTS, NAILS, HAIR	KESTREL, ROBIN, PELICAN	ESOPHAGUS, INTESTINE, MOUTH	PITCHER, UMPIRE, FANS	PENS, PENCILS, MARKERS
CASH REGISTER, PANTS, CLERKS	CANOES, SURFBOARDS, LOGS	LUNGE, TRACHEA, NOSE	TELLERS, VAULT, MONEY	CHIMPS, BATS, LEMURS
SWALLOW, ORIOLE, PARROT	DISHES, GLASSES, PLATES	JALAPEÑOS, SALSA, SAUCES	FILLING, DRILL, TOOTHBRUSH	CAMERA, REMOTE CONTROL, RADIO
EAST, NORTH, WEST	HAWK, PIGEON, DOVE	CHOCOLATE, BRAN, CORN	ZIP CODE, NAME, STATE	CAR, CHECK, CHARGE
PENGUIN, HERON, WARBLER	TUESDAY, FRIDAY, MONDAY	WEIGHTS, BARS, TOWELS	VEGETABLE, ONION, CHICKEN NOODLE	PAPERS, FINGERNAILS, BILLS
LUGGAGE, PASSPORT, TICKETS	THE SUN, SCHOOL BUS, LEMON	PHEASANT, OWL, DUCK	MISSOURI, MONTANA, LOUISIANA	MACHINERY, CONCEPTS, STATIC

Category for leftover words: birds
Other items that fit the category: ostrich,
toucan, swan

Details to Main Idea to Details 1 (Page 85)

RUSSIAN	CATS	BUS	CARAMEL	BASKETBALL
SUMMER	SOLITAIRE	JELLY BEANS	HAT	AIRPLANE
APRIL	DAISY	TENT	DIVER	FIBULA
FUCHSIA	TRUCK	FRY	YO-YO	MONKEY
FORK	PIGGY BANK	TRAIN	SCIENCE	SCALLOP
SUNTAN LOTION	SKIS	LEAVES	PIANO KEYS	GRANDMOTHER
JET	CHECKERS	SOFA	LIPSTICK	SUBWAY
OVEN	HAMMER	OSTRICH	TYPHOON	BROCCOLI
TOUCHDOWN	SAPPHIRE	CD-ROM DRIVE	WATERMELON	FIFTY

Possible categories: transportation, vehicles,
things you can ride in, things that take you
from one place to another
Other items that fit the category: car, rocket,
space shuttle, motor home, motorcycle,
bicycle, skateboard

Details to Main Idea to Details 2 (Page 90)

TONGUE	NORTH AMERICA	SWIM	PANCAKES	QUART
TUESDAY	JUMP	ADJECTIVES	"EXIT"	TEACHER
WINTER	SHEEP	TANGO	FLOUR	SWISS
PLANES	READ	PEACH	CHEESE	TITANIUM
BUDDIES	SWEATER	RATTLESNAKE	SNICKERDOODLES	RYE
HEXAGON	HAT	SALAD DRESSING	BUILD	BEDROOM
RUN	POODLE	HERMIT CRAB	TENT	RESERVATIONS
RIDE	STEM	OAK	PROTEIN	CLAM CHOWDER
OPOSSUMS	KIDNEY	TAKING OUT THE TRASH	SODA	DISAPPOINTED

Possible categories: activities, things to do
Other items that fit the category: dig, gallop,
crawl, stretch, write, leap, catch, hit, throw,
swing, twist

Plural Nouns (Page 95)

CHILDREN	THIEVES	CHEFS	SANDWICHES	BOXES
MICE	MATCHES	DEER	WISHES	LOAVES
WHAT	SHEEP	TEETH	LIVES	LABS
KEYS	DID	BUNNIES	THE	CHEWING
RINGS	SKIES	WATCHES	CALVES	GEESE
GUM	SAY TO	LUNCHES	THE	FEET
HALVES	SHOE	SHELVES	I'M	LEAVES
STUCK	WIVES	BUSES	KISSES	ON YOU
MEN	CUPS	MOOSE	OXEN	BUSHES
WOMEN	OWLS	TAXES	FISH	CLOCKS

Answers will vary, but each sentence must
include a plural noun from the list.

Changing Present- to Past-Tense Verbs 1 (Page 100)

FLEW	SANK	SENT	WHAT'S	TAUGHT
THREW	BLACK	SOLD	DRANK	AND
WHITE	TOLD	TORE	BUILT	PAID
BROUGHT	AND	BENT	SAID	DREW
ATE	LIT	PINK	SHOOK	SANG
ALL	HUNG	RAN	OVER	FORGAVE
GREW	CRIED	LED	AN	BIT
TOOK	BLEW	CAUGHT	KNEW	WORE
GAVE	EMBARRASSED	WROTE	FED	SPENT
LENT	MADE	ZEBRA	RANG	CLUNG

Answers will vary, but each sentence must
include a past-tense verb from the list.

Changing Present- to Past-Tense Verbs 2 (Page 105)

WEPT	BOUGHT	FOUND	MET	LOST
HELD	DID	WHY	WROTE	LAY
DO	DROVE	CHOSE	SWEPT	BIRDS
DOVE	FOUGHT	FLY	LED	GREW
SPOKE	FILED	RODE	ATE	SPED
THOUGHT	CALLED	SOUTH	CHARGED	BECAUSE
IT'S	GOT	RANG	TOO	BLED
WENT	BLEW	LAUGHED	CREPT	WOKE
FAR	SMASHED	BROKE	TO	KEPT
SLEPT	WALK	FROZE	SANG	KNEW

Answers will vary, but each sentence must
include a past-tense verb from the list.

Comparative and Superlative Adjectives (Page 110)

FASTER	CHEAPER	BRIGHTER	SHINIEST	PRETTIER
MESSIEST	BIGGER	MEANER	FURRIEST	WHAT
DO	FUNNIER	FUNNIEST	YOU	FASTEST
NEATEST	SMARTER	SMARTEST	BRIGHTEST	CALL
A	SCARED	DIRTIEST	WISER	NICER
BIGGEST	KINDEST	SHORTER	DIRTIER	DINOSAUR
THINNER	MESSIER	TALLER	CHEAPEST	PRETTIEST
THINNEST	NICEST	WISEST	HEAVIEST	SOFTER
MEANEST	SHINIER	CLEANEST	A	CUTER
HEAVIER	NERVOUS	TALLEST	Rex	.

Answers will vary, but each sentence must include a comparative or superlative adjective from the list.

Nouns, Verbs, and Adjectives (Page 115)

CLIPPED	PLAY	DELICATE	HUGE	DOG
COLD	PARK	WHY	BUNNY	STICKY
ARE	RECYCLE	BULLDOZER	BOTTLE	CHECK
MESSY	NOISY	SOCKS	TEDDY	FOUND
BEARS	TRAIN	TIRED	NEVER	RUSHED
CALL	EXPENSIVE	HUNGRY	EAT	RABBIT
BECAUSE	BOOK	RACKET	THEY	POUR
DEPARTED	ARE	CLOUDY	EMPTY	ICE CREAM
BALL	FELL	STORMY	ALWAYS	JACKET
STUFFED	COLORFUL	PAINTED	ADORABLE	SEE

Answers will vary, but each sentence must include a noun from the list.

Pronouns, Adjectives, and Adverbs (Page 120)

RARELY	BRAVELY	INFLATED	THEY	REGRETFULLY
IT	RAPIDLY	FILTHY	HAPPILY	WHAT
DID	QUIETLY	NEATLY	RECYCLED	HE
CAREFULLY	THE	LOUDLY	THEM	SPIDER
SLOWLY	I	SHE	PROMPTLY	PROUDLY
DO	TIRED	ON	THOUGHTFULLY	THE
QUICKLY	WE	YOU	EASILY	SHORTLY
WHEAT	LATE	COMPUTER	HIM	MADE
ORGANIZED	A	FEROCIOUS	SILENTLY	BROKEN
SPICY	BRIGHT	WEBSITE	DELICIOUS	ANXIOUSLY

Answers will vary, but each sentence must include a pronoun, an adjective, or an adverb from the list.

Parts of Speech (Page 125)

HAMMERS	WHAT	INTO	QUIETLY	QUICKLY
DID	AROUND	POURED	THE	CAUTIOUSLY
RARE	SHARP	RARELY	GROUND	THROUGH
BALD	SAY	RUSHED	ABOUT	COW
SHE	WE	WATCH	SYMMETRICAL	FOLLOWED
OR	FROZEN	TO THE	SLOWLY	OVER
AND	THEY	DUSTED	EARTHQUAKE	HEALTHY
UNDER	PLAYED	YOU	HE	ON
CRACK	SPOKE	VACANT	BEFORE	DAMP
SMELLY	FEET	ME	NEAR	UP

Answers will vary, but each sentence must include a word from the list and the nouns, verbs, and adjectives should be correctly marked.

Prepositions and Conjunctions (Page 130)

BETWEEN	WHY	FROM	DID	AND
THE	UNLESS	COOKIE	AS LONG AS	GO
WHENEVER	DURING	OVER	OUTSIDE	UNTIL
TOWARD	IF	BESIDE	ABOUT	TO
THE	OFF	UNDER	BECAUSE	ALTHOUGH
HOSPITAL	BEHIND	AT	BUT	IT
INTO	UNDERNEATH	OTHERWISE	HOWEVER	INSIDE
FELT	ON	OR	DOWN	CRUMBY
UP	WHILE	AROUND	ABOVE	INSTEAD OF
NEAR	OF	SO	BELOW	YET

Answers will vary, but each sentence must include a preposition or conjunction from the list, and each should be correctly marked.

Homophones 1 (Page 135)

WHO	BLEW	AD	WALKS	SUM
ADD	WASTE	DEW	WRITE	IN
THREW	THE	CENT	SCENT	CORD
DUE	CHORD	WEAR	TWO	WOOD
HEIR	WOODS	AIR	ANTS	ATE
BLUE	TALE	RIGHT	WITH	AUNTS
NOTHING	WOULD	TOO	AXE	CARROT
ACTS	ON	THROUGH	EIGHT	A
HARE	CARET	SENT	BARE	THRONE
THROWN	BEAR	HAIR	TO	SOME

Answers will vary. Possible answers include:
She ate eight cookies for dessert.
He blew out the five blue candles on the cake.
The new student had some trouble calculating the sum for the addition problem.

Homophones 2 (Page 140)

HALL	NO	WHAT'S	MAID	HEAL
RAIN	EARN	FARE	REIGN	AN
EQUINE	CREATURE	STEAL	PIER	LEAD
STARE	PIECE	STEEL	LEAST	LED
LOSING	PALE	PAUSE	LEASED	ITS
KNOW	FUR	MADE	URN	PEER
VOICE	HEEL	CALLED	HAUL	MAIL
NOSE	PEACE	KERNEL	TACKS	A
TAX	HOARSE	PAIL	FAIR	STAIR
FIR	PAWS	COLONEL	HORSE	MALE

Answers will vary.

Similes 1 (Page 145)

GHOST	WHERE	PIE	SKUNK	SHOULD
LARK	EEL	ICE	BEE	MULE
SUGAR	MOUSE	SKY	BIRD	YOU
WHISTLE	NEVER	WEED	TURTLE	TACK
TAKE	BUG IN A RUG	A	BONE	JET
PANCAKE	DOG	MONKEY	TO	ARROW
SUN	SILK	BABY	OX	LAMB
A	BOARD	BARREL	SWAN	FEATHER
BEAR	FROG	FLEA	LION	MARKET
FOX	ROCK	LEAF	RAINBOW	BUTTON

Answers will vary. Possible answers include:
She sings like a lark.
He was as hungry as a tiger.

Similes 2 (Page 150)

SWAN	FUR	MUD	HATTER	PEACOCK
HOW ARE	PANCAKE	TIGERS	NIGHT	LIKE
OWL	DOG	ROSES	SERGEANTS	LARK
DOORNAIL	IN	RAIL	GIRAFFE	BUS
THE	JAM	ARMY	FLOWER	HAWK
MULE	FLASH	SHEEP'S CLOTHING	GRASS	KITTEN
BAT	PIGSTY	THEY	BOTH	MOLASSES
GOOSE	HAVE	LIGHTNING	NAILS	QUEEN
STRIPES	FIDDLE	BIRD	HERD OF ELEPHANTS	CUCUMBER
BOX OF CRAYONS	CHURCH MOUSE	NEEDLE	SAHARA DESERT	BEAVER

Answers will vary. Possible answers include:
He was as curious as a cat looking in a hole.
She felt out of place like a fish out of water.

Idioms (Page 155)

I'M TIRED	IT'S SO EASY.	I UNDERSTAND.	HE DID VERY WELL.	HELP ME.
YOU NEED TO BE QUIET.	WHEN	YOU NEED TO BE PATIENT.	HE TALKS SO FAST!	IS
WE HAD A VERY DIFFICULT DECISION TO MAKE.	I'LL TELL YOU MY OPINION.	IT'S TIME TO STUDY.	THE	SHE'S BOTHERING ME.
I WOULD TAKE A RISK TO HELP YOU.	VETERINARIAN	TRY NOT TO RUSH INTO SOMETHING TOO QUICKLY.	HE GOT IN TROUBLE AND WAS BEING PUNISHED.	
SHE'S THE BOSS.	SHE IS CONSTANTLY CHANGING HER MIND.	LET'S GO EAT.	HE WANTS TO PAY.	YOU'LL BE AMAZED.
I'M READY TO LISTEN CAREFULLY.	THE BUSIEST	HE FINISHED AT THE LAST POSSIBLE MOMENT.	YOU HAVE A PROBLEM AND DON'T HAVE AN EASY SOLUTION.	WHEN
HURRY.	HE OWED MORE MONEY THAN HE HAD.	IT'S BEDTIME.	YOU TOOK ON MORE TASKS THAN YOU COULD HANDLE.	SHE WAS SICK.
SHE THOUGHT IT WAS FUNNY.	I'M DEPRESSED TODAY.	IT'S	RAINING	CATS
LEAVE ME ALONE.	IT'S VERY EXPENSIVE.	I AM GOING TO GET AN A.	I NEED YOU TO HELP.	YOU NEED TO STOP.
I ATE TOO MUCH.	AND	KEEP HOPING.	DOGS	SHE DOESN'T EAT MUCH.

Answers will vary.

Meaning to Root/Prefix/Suffix (Page 160)

BENE, BEN, AND BON	DICT	RE-	AUTO-	MIS AND MIT
HE WHO	VIS	STRUCT	HYPO-	CRED
GRAPH, SCRIB, AND SCRIPT	IS NOT	METER AND METRY	TRACT	RUPT
SATISFIED	TERR, TERRA, AND GEO	WITH A	POST-	-OLOGY
PHON, PHONO, AND PHONE	THERM	TRANS-	JECT	VERS AND VERT
JUR, JUS, AND JUD	-PHOBIA	CEDE, CEED, AND CESS	LITTLE	TRI-
QUAD-	WILL	MICRO-	FLECT AND FLEX	BIO, VIT, AND VIV
NOT	PORT	CIRC- AND CIRCUM-	BE	SATISFIED
MORPH	SECT	HYPER-	WITH	MONO- AND UNI-
NAV, NAUS, AND NAUT	NEG	SOCIO	PRE	A LOT

Possible answers: The proverb means that to be happy in life you must first be happy with yourself. Having a lot does not make a person happy.

Root/Prefix/Suffix to Meaning (Page 165)

TO JOIN, MEET, OR LINK	ROOT	GOOD OR WELL	NOVUS	LAW OR JUSTICE
WRITE OR WRITING	ORDO	TO BIND, TIE, OR DRAW TIGHT	TO SEE OR LOOK	SECLORUM
WHICH	THE STUDY OF	MEANS	TO BEND	TWO
TO BREAK	WITHOUT	AGAINST OR OPPOSITE	LAND OR EARTH	TO THROW
TO SPEAK	HEAT OR TEMPERATURE	BAD, ABNORMAL, OR WORSE	TOGETHER OR WITH	BAD OR BADLY, WRONG, OR ILL
WITHIN	ONE	TOGETHER OR WITH	HAND	UNDER OR BELOW
A	ABLE TO BE	ACROSS	FRIEND OR COMPANION	TO TURN
BEFORE	NEW	A FEAR OF	TO GO OR YIELD	TO CUT OR SEPARATE
ORDER	TO BELIEVE	FOR	TO BUILD	NOT OR NONE
LIFE OR LIVE	THE	AFTER	AGES	AGAIN

Answers will vary. Possible answer: The dollar represents the currency in a new united land.

Proverbs (Page 170)

FLOCK TOGETHER	SKIN DEEP	TANGO	EAT IT TOO	BOWL OF CHERRIES
NOTHING	THAN NEVER	MEDICINE	THAN ONE	GO ROUND
BEFORE THEY HATCH	ALL EVILS	MAKE A RIGHT	LOST	ARE FREE
VENTURED	MAY FLOWERS	NOTHING	CHOOSERS	VIRTUE
THE MICE WILL PLAY	OUT OF MIND	BELIEVING	GAINED	THERE IS A WAY
YOU LOSE SOME	IN THE MOUTH	MEANS THAT	THAN WORDS	IS BLISS
LEAP	YOU WILL NEVER	SORRY	SUCCEED	HEART GROW FONDER
A DULL BOY	ON THE OTHER SIDE OF THE FENCE	FAST	KEEPS THE DOCTOR AWAY	IN ANYTHING
PERFECT	UNLESS YOU	IS NOT GOLD	ARE WILLING	FRIEND INDEED
THINK ALIKE	TO TRY	WATER	HEAR NO LIES	LOSERS WEEPERS

Answers will vary.

Critical Thinking and Deduction 1 (Page 175)

NOSE	LAMP	TEETH	STAMP	SOCKS
BANANA	CATALOG	TOOTHPASTE	ANIMAL	ANCHOR
EYE	THEATER	PIANO	TENNIS	HAIR
COFFEE	BOOK	TRAIN	RADIO	BACKPACK
NEEDLE	BEAR	THERMOMETER	CLOCK	IMAGINATION
BICYCLE	VIOLIN	CLOUDS	ORANGUTAN	SCISSORS
TAPE	LEMON	BIRD	PLANE	BANK
RABBIT	PAJAMAS	PIE	SODA	KEY
CORN	ORGAN	ANTS	CAMERA	LIBRARY
UMBRELLA	BEACH	SNAKE	CARROT	SALAD

CARNIVOROUS
Clues will vary. Possible clues include:
1. It describes most large cats.
2. It describes eating habits.
3. It's the word that describes how some animals eat that is the opposite of herbivores.

Critical Thinking and Deduction 2 (Page 180)

PENCIL	PRESIDENT	TENT	FLAG	PURSE
BUNNY	BOWLING	MANDIBLE	CASTLE	APPLE
YACHT	FIREPLACE	WATCH	NEWSPAPER	ICE CREAM
ONION	CAMEL	VOLCANO	HONEY	CAKE
FLASHLIGHT	TURNIP	TREE	OXEN	SANDWICH
SNAKE	COMPUTER	RUBBER	WINTER	EGGS
CELL PHONE	CLOWN	KING	MIRROR	PAINTING
HORSE	MONEY	YOLK	PERFUME	BUCKET
CLARINET	HEART	LEMUR	ICE	STORM
EMERALD	ELEPHANT	BASKETBALL	FORK	SURPRISE

MOTORCYCLES
Clues will vary. Possible clues include:
1. They are vehicles.
2. You should wear a helmet while on them.
3. They usually have two wheels.

Oxymorons (Page 185)

WHOLE PIECE	PEOPLE WHO	LOUD WHISPER	DON'T LIKE	JUMBO SHRIMP
SIT UP	LEAST FAVORITE	WAKING UP	MEAN SMILE	POSITIVELY WRONG
SUMMER SCHOOL	COLD SWEAT	FREEZER BURN	SILENT ALARM	INVISIBLE INK
DRY ICE	CALM STORM	IN THE MORNING	CURVED LINES	ONE CHOICE
SAY THAT	HOME OFFICE	PERFECTLY RIDICULOUS	ACT NATURALLY	SUGARLESS CANDY
BLACK LIGHT	TURNED UP MISSING	THE	NEVER AGAIN	PHRASE
SAD CLOWN	ORGANIZED CHAOS	HONEST LIAR	SMALL FORTUNE	LOOSE KNOT
"GOOD MORNING"	MINOR CATASTROPHE	IS	OLD NEWS	SHARP CURVES
LONG SHORTS	AN	INSIDE OUT	SERIOUS FUN	TERRIBLY CUTE
SLUMBER PARTY	CLEARLY MISUNDERSTOOD	OXYMORON	POWER NAP	ORIGINAL COPY

Answers will vary. Possible answer: They might say that "Good morning" is an oxymoron because they would rather sleep in than wake up in the morning.

Answers will vary. Possible answer: The term "mild jalapeño" would be an oxymoron because jalapeños are spicy and hot and therefore are not mild.

Associative Connections 1 (Page 190)

WHITE	BANDANA	DOGS	EXIT	TURN
ROLL	CONTRAST	ORANGES	CLARK	RACECAR
POTATOES	RESCUE	FOR ALL	FORGET	BEYOND
SUGAR	Mr. HYDE	EAGLE	HOUSE OF REPRESENTATIVES	ARMY
DREAM	THIN	EFFECT	BUSTLE	CENTS
FAUNA	PEPPER	SOUTH	CREAM CHEESE	HAM
DEMOCRAT	STRIPES	BADMINTON	FOUND	UMPIRE
BALL	TAXES	EVEN	SQUARE	DEBIT
ROBBERS	FAMOUS	RIGHT	COLD	TIRE
ENVELOPE	WEST	RAINCOAT	SOCKS	SAUCERS

BREAD and BUTTER
Answers will vary. Possible answers include: toothpaste and toothbrush, topic sentence and concluding sentence, hot and cold, tea and biscuits.

Associative Connections 2 (Page 195)

John Smith	COCKROACH	SOUND	TRUE	GRAVY
BLUE	DEATH	LADYBUG	ENDS	SELL
SPICE	BUTTER	CONS	THANK YOU	PENCIL
LOSERS	ONION	SNIFF	TELL	LEARN
SHOULDERS	FORTH	CONDITIONER	STONES	PEACE
GENTLEMEN	APPLE	LIGHTNING	A LEG	WATER
KANGAROO	VERTICAL	DOG	MEATBALLS	LOSS
NEEDLES	WRONG	APE	BOLTS	FALSE
GARDEN	GRAPES	ROBIN	GRETEL	CRACKERS
JELLY	BOTTOM	EMU	ROOSTER	EARLY

CLOAK and DAGGER
Answers will vary. Possible answers include: highs and lows, ups and downs, twists and turns.

Clichés (Page 200)

TONGUE	YOUR ALLEY	PULL A	NEVER	LUCK
THE LIMIT	IN IT	ARE TURNED	OUT	THE DRAW
FAST	SHADE	ONE	EARTH	HEELS
MY THROAT	A NEW LEAF	FITS ALL	MEANS	FIRE
THAT	EYE	TREE	ON EGGSHELLS	OTHER CHEEK
MATTER	ROUTE	PENNY	OF TIME	A PERSON
TRIES TO	THIN ICE	DAY	THE CHARM	CUP OF TEA
WEAR IT	TRICK	THE BELL	THUMBS	AND
DOUBLE-CROSS	OF THE CROP	BY A HAIR	HIS GRAVE	SINCE SLICED BREAD
A STAR	SOMEONE	CASE	HOLE	BOAT

Answers will vary.
Possible answer: The cliché "time flies when you're having fun" means when you are enjoying yourself time seems to go by quickly.
Possible answer: The cliché "cool as a cucumber" describes someone who stays calm during a tense or stressful situation.

Notes

Notes